The Cultural World of the Prophets

The Cultural World of the Prophets

The First Reading and the Responsorial Psalm

Sunday by Sunday,
Year B

John J. Pilch

THE LITURGICAL PRESS
Collegeville, Minnesota

www.litpress.org

Cover design by David Manahan, O.S.B. Photo courtesy of The Liturgical Press Archives.

1   2   3   4   5   6   7   8   9

ISBN 0-8146-2787-0

In loving memory of
Rev. Serafin Stanisław Potoczny, O.F.M.
my saintly cousin,
Manasterz, Poland
and
Rev. Jan Marcin Długosz, O.F.M.
professor, friend, and mentor,
Dąbrowa, Poland

Contents

Introduction

When I wrote *The Cultural World of Jesus Sunday by Sunday* (3 vols., The Liturgical Press, 1995–97), I resolved to write a companion series: *The Cultural World of the Apostles: The Second Reading Sunday by Sunday* (3 vols., The Liturgical Press, 2001–03). My intention was to provide the average person with a handy study guide first for the gospel readings, then later for the second readings in the liturgy every Sunday which are drawn chiefly from letters. Since it was becoming— and still is—increasingly difficult for adults to find some free time during the week to attend a study group or lecture series on the Bible, I thought that a six-hundred word essay on the Scripture heard at liturgy on Sunday could be manageable and interesting. A person could read that while sitting in the pew before the liturgy began. If the homily wasn't working out well, a person could read the reflection in its place.

That the booklets have been useful for preachers, catechists, liturgists, and others as well came as a pleasant and welcome surprise. My publisher's suggestion to write a series on the first readings in the liturgy Sunday by Sunday, *The Cultural World of the Prophets,* also came as a surprise. The gospels and the second readings in Sunday liturgies present selections in a continuous or semi-continuous sequence that facilitates an orderly study of a gospel or a letter of an apostle Sunday by Sunday.

In contrast, the selection and arrangement of the first readings in Sunday liturgies do not lend themselves to a similar study program. Yet the Old Testament passages are of significance in Christian worship. With this volume I turn to the task of offering insight into these Old Testament passages, a task of interest to me since graduate school. At the beginning of the second year in my first teaching position after completing my degree with a specialty in the New Testament (the letters of Paul), the dean asked if I could teach Old Testament courses. If not, my year-to-year contract would not be renewed, since he had just hired a Harvard graduate to teach New Testament and now needed someone to teach Old Testament. Well, of course I could teach the Old Testament! My graduate training at Marquette University was quite broad compared to other institutions. My Old Testament teachers included J. Coert Rylersdaam, Roland Murphy, o.carm., Robert North, s.j., Thomas Caldwell, s.j., John F. X. Sheehan, s.j., and Gordon Bahr, among others. An article I published in *Harvard Theological Review* as a graduate student critically reviewed a scholarly study of Martin Luther's *Commentaries on the Psalms*. In all the years that have passed since beginning the serious study of Scripture, I have maintained a balanced interest in the entire Bible.

As a rule, the first reading—mainly though not always from the Old Testament—has been chosen in order to harmonize, in a more or less explicit way, with the doctrine and events recounted in the gospel. At times the connection is very slim, and in addition to that, the selections are drawn from all over the Old Testament. The readings are neither continuous nor semi-continuous. Biblical scholars and liturgists have lamented that the Old Testament does not get a fair hearing in the liturgy. From a modern, historically oriented point of view, this is correct. The gospel controls the selection of the first reading in Sunday liturgies. There is no escaping the impression that the gospel is considered more important in our worship service. That conviction, however, has some ancient roots. Theodore Abu Qurrah, Bishop of Haran (d. ninth century c.e.), the town from where Abraham departed for Canaan, wrote:

> Were it not for the Gospel, we would not have acknowledged Moses to be from God. Rather, on reflection, we would have vigorously opposed him. Likewise, we have

acknowledged the prophets to be from God because of the Gospel. It is not on the basis of reason, since we have acknowledged them because Christ has informed us that they are prophets. Also, because we have knowledge of Christ's whole economy, and having read their books and discovered that they had previously described his whole economy just as he accomplished it, we have acknowledged that they are prophets. At this point in time we do not acknowledge Christ and his affairs because of the books of the prophets. Rather, we acknowledge them because of Christ's saying that they are prophets and because of our own recognition that his economy is written in their books.[1]

Just as in the volumes of my other The Cultural World of . . . series, so too here I present the reader with a thumbnail sketch of the literary context and historical setting of each Scripture text segment as it contributes to understanding the selected verses. I also present cultural information, at length when necessary (for example, see the discussion of Leviticus 13 on the Sixth Sunday in Ordinary Time), which is indispensable for understanding those verses appropriately and which is usually unavailable in other commentaries or resources. That kind of cultural information is what has made this series distinctive. I include similar brief reflections on the Responsorial Psalm, and for each Sunday I indicate the apparent link ("more or less explicit") by which the gospel should be associated with the first reading. There may indeed be links or associations other than those I have indicated. Finally, the Sundays marked with an asterisk (*) were assigned readings that are repeated in each year of the lectionary cycle. I will repeat these reflections substantially unchanged in the other volumes of this series just as I did in the volumes of the previous series.

I am grateful to The Liturgical Press for publishing and promoting my cultural reflections and to the readers around

[1] Quoted from Bruce J. Malina, "Three Theses for a More Adequate Reading of the New Testament," *Practical Theology: Perspectives from the Plains,* ed. Michael G. Lawler and Gail S. Risch (Omaha: Creighton University Press, 2000) 33–60.

the world who continue to welcome and to benefit from these publications. I believe that together, we all have taken some important steps toward realizing a goal that I set for myself upon completing my graduate studies: to contribute toward improving preaching.

Feast of Blessed Simon   John J. Pilch
   of Lipnica, O.F.M. CONV. (Poland)   Georgetown University
July 18, 2001   and the University of
                                                          Pretoria, South Africa

First Sunday of Advent
Isaiah 63:16b-17, 19b; 64:2-7

All the Old Testament readings for the Sundays of Advent speak of the Messiah. The majority are drawn from the prophet Isaiah. Today's verses from Third Isaiah are part of a community lament sung sometime after the return from Exile. The lament (63:8–64:4a) is followed by a confession and appeal to God (64:4b-6). The community laments its predicament. The return from Exile has been disappointing. It has not fulfilled their hopes. The Temple is still in ruins. Whose fault is it? They recognize and admit it is theirs, of course! "We are sinful . . .; / There is none who calls upon your name, / who rouses himself to cling to you." Why do they behave like this? That's God's fault! "Why do you . . . harden our hearts so that we fear you not?" What can God do to remedy this? "Rend the heavens and come down." These returnees seek a theophany even more wonderful than that of Sinai (see Exodus 19). At Jesus' baptism, this will indeed occur: the heavens will be rent and God will speak (Mark 1:10), but at this moment in history, the returnees can only hope to stir God by their confession of guilt to become present among them again.

They liken their sinful condition to a very serious and shameful cultural breach of purity, that of a woman in her period ("all our good deeds are like polluted rags"; see Lev 15:19-24). While in modern Western culture this is a normal experience for women, in ancient Israel it was a polluting condition that made one unclean. The experience required physical separation from the community and from the community's God; it also called for purification so that one might resume one's place in community and before God. The involuntary condition constituted a failure to be holy and pure as God is holy and pure.

As serious as the condition of sin, alienation from God, might be, these people pray for perseverance in their resolve to reform and serve God faithfully: "Would that you might meet us doing right, / that we were mindful of you in our ways" (Isa 64:5). This notion links the first reading with today's gospel (Mark 13:33-37): "May he [the lord of the household, or the Lord] not come suddenly and find you sleeping. . . . Watch!"

Responsorial Psalm: 80:2-3, 15-16, 18-19

The sentiments of these selected psalm verses complement the first reading rather well. The psalm reflects the period of the Assyrian invasion of Israel, the northern kingdom, either in 733/32 or 722/21 B.C.E. Despite the experience of shocking loss and devastation in these historical circumstances, Israelites stand firm in their loyalty to God. They plead for God to look after the planted vine (Isa 5:1-7; Ezek 15:1-8), to rouse divine power and come to save them. "Give us new life, and we will call upon your name." What is the basis of this fidelity to God? The Jerusalem Temple still stands. Perhaps some shrines in the north still survive. The refrain of this psalm, which is also the refrain of this response, highlights the people's consciousness of God being present in the Temple services in Jerusalem yet painfully absent in the national life at this time in the northern kingdom.

Second Sunday of Advent
Isaiah 40:1-5, 9-11

These verses from the first of seventeen lyrical and persua-
sive speeches by Second Isaiah (40–55) are carefully balanced. The scene is set in a heavenly assembly. In an altered
state of consciousness, the prophet makes a sky journey to
this assembly. In such divine assemblies, God determines
what must happen on earth. In contrast, assemblies of pagan
gods were raucous, often dominated by a vocal minority. They
usually ended in an uneasy compromise between the parties.
Here, the Lord God is in charge. Second Isaiah is directed
(v. 2) to console Israel now that she is exiled in Babylon.
Through the prophet God announced that Israel is forgiven.

Verses 3-5 set the pattern for verses 9-11. The prophet cries
out (v. 3) God's command to prepare a highway for God
(vv. 4-5). The imagery is familiar from leveling a bumpy road:
ruts (valleys) are filled in and bumps (hills) are made low
(leveled). The glory, honor, or reputation of the Lord will be
revealed on this road. Zion/Jerusalem also is to announce in
a loud voice (v. 9) the coming of the Lord with might. The
Lord will be surrounded with royal glory while leading the
exiles back to Jerusalem (vv. 10-11).

Anyone who has visited the Middle East knows that its
deserts are not just sand but especially places of mountains
and deep valleys. Think of the Dead Sea region, Qumran,
Jericho, Beer Sheba. They are sterile places whose death-
dealing character makes them unfit for human life. But God
levels the hills, lays down a road, brings in water, and makes

3

the place habitable. What was once entirely lifeless is now the seat of the glory of the Lord!

Creation and exodus themes are readily apparent in these verses. When God speaks, peace results. Heavenly messengers obey, earthly messengers are appointed. Zion/Jerusalem is the place where the Lord resumes residence.

This reading is linked to the gospel (Mark 1:1-8) by the verse Mark adapts from Isaiah. The prophet said to prepare the way of the Lord in the desert. Mark (1:3) says: a voice cries out in the desert (likely John the Baptist): prepare the way of the Lord. Our ancestors in the faith regularly made creative applications of their traditions.

Responsorial Psalm: 85:9-10, 11-12, 13-14

The central verses of this psalm selected for today's liturgy very likely date from the early days after the return from exile. Israel has learned its lesson. The glorious promises of Second Isaiah have not been fulfilled. During the first years back in the land, Israel experienced drought and poor crops (Haggai; Zechariah 1-8; Isaiah 56-59). The repetition of certain words (e.g., land, peace, justice) reflect covenant themes. Israel is pleading with God to reinstate the covenant bond that manifests the reliability of God's good will, kindness, and faithfulness.

Third Sunday of Advent
Isaiah 61:1-2a, 10-11

Chapters 60–62 of Third Isaiah (56–66) were very likely written by a devoted disciple of Second Isaiah. Isaiah 61:1-2 echoes the servant songs of Second Isaiah: anointing by the spirit (42:1) for a ministry of mercy (42:2-3, 6-7); a "jubilee year" or year of favor (49:8). As noted in Leviticus 25, such a jubilee year was proclaimed every fifty years for the purpose of having debts canceled, granting general forgiveness, and for recovering lost property. These words are spoken by the prophet himself. That he declares himself anointed is an interesting point. While Ezekiel made much of the spirit anointment of priests so that they would prophesy, Third Isaiah extends the spirit's activity beyond royalty and the priesthood to the laity who will be named "priests of the Lord" (vv. 4-6; Exod 19:6; 1 Pet 2:5). In verses 9-11, Jerusalem speaks and revels in the restoration and fulfillment of love between herself and YHWH (54:5-8; Jer 33:10-11). Careful readers will distinguish the two speakers in these paired verses (1-2 and 10-11).

Curiously, the verses omitted from this reading (vv. 4-6) make the best link with the gospel, where John, the son of a priest, decided not to take up his inherited status but rather takes on the prophet's mantle to critique the aristocratic Jerusalem priesthood.

Responsorial Psalm: Luke 1:46-48, 49-50, 53-54

The familiar words of Mary's poetry are appointed as the responsorial psalm for this reading with the refrain echoing

Isaiah 61:10b as the lectionary indicates. A key idea in these verses is reversal: the hungry are fed, the greedy (this is the usual meaning of "rich" in the Bible; people who refuse to share their surplus) are sent away empty. This is a common theme in ancient near eastern literature and in the Old Testament whence Mary's poem draws its inspiration. This is a fitting response to the reading from Third Isaiah in which Jerusalem proudly announced its own reversal of bad to good fortune.

Fourth Sunday of Advent
2 Samuel 7:1-5, 8b-12, 14a, 16

This passage is one of three forms (see Psalm 89 and 1 Chronicles 17) in which Nathan's oracle concerning the foundation of Davidic messianism has been recorded. In 2 Samuel, Nathan uses a clever play on words to deliver his message. While David intended to build a "house" (Hebrew: *bayith*) for the Lord, namely the Ark, the Lord will instead build a "house" or dynasty *(bayith)* for him. This dynasty is God's chosen human agent of salvation in human history. In Nathan's oracle, salvation is presented as political achievement to be wrought by a successor to David. Luke's allusion to this passage in today's gospel (Luke 1:26-38) expands its meaning. Just as God watched over David, the head of the dynasty, so does God watch over Jesus, successor to David in the dynasty.

Responsorial Psalm: 89:2-3, 4-5, 27, 29

This psalm is a liturgical lament over a military defeat. Any such defeat is viewed as a threat that would jeopardize God's promises to David. The verses selected for today reflect chiefly on God's steadfast love and fidelity, which guarantee the endurance and success of David's dynasty and God's plan.

Verses 2-5 form a solid unit. An "inclusion" (repetition of words or phrases signaling the beginning and end of a unit) is marked by the words "forever" and "all generations." Moreover, the words "establish" and "confirm" are so situated in their verses as to form a chiasm (an "X" shaped arrangement of words or phrases called a chiasm because the name of the Greek letter "X" is chi), further strengthening the unit. The idea: God's steadfast love and fidelity are quite visible in creation and in the Davidic dynasty. Verses 4 and 5 clearly borrow from 2 Samuel 7. Verse 27 repeats the ideas of 2 Samuel 7:14, and verse 29 affirms the lasting nature of the dynasty. The psalm refrain is a very suitable response to the goodness of YHWH upon which the lamenting nation knows it can always count.

* Vigil of the Nativity
Isaiah 62:1-5

These verses appear to capture the prophet's meditation on chapters that Second Isaiah, his master, had composed (Isaiah 40; 51; 54). In these verses Third Isaiah sings about Israel rising to new life from its destruction. The imagery that dominates these verses is drawn from espousals. Zion/Jerusalem's good fortune will break forth as suddenly and brightly as a desert dawn. In antiquity, deities often wore a crown that imitated the walls of their city on earth. Here God is holding such a crown; God is indeed in charge of this glorious restoration. One of the names by which the city once could be described ("forsaken") is the name of a queen-mother (*Azuba;* 1 Kgs 22:42). Cities were considered to be feminine. The new names carry similar symbolism. For example, "my delight" *(Hephzibah)* is another queen-mother (2 Kgs 21:1), but the names portray a reversal of destiny. The forsaken woman (city) is now God's delight. This is especially evident in the name "espoused" *(beʿula)*, which forgets Israel's whoring ways as described by Hosea 2:18.

In this culture, an unfaithful wife would have to be set aside or killed (see Num 5:11-31; Deut 22:13-21). The ideal marriage partner is a patrilateral cousin. What if there is no other available female cousin to replace the unfaithful partner? The man would have to remain unmarried and alone. In the real world of this culture, it is preferable to swallow one's pride, bear the shame, and keep the faithless partner than to be absolutely correct but lose one's partner. So, too, with

God. Since all God-talk is based upon and rooted in human experience culturally conditioned, God can be expected to swallow pride, put up with the disappointment, and, as the prophet says, "as a young man marries a virgin, / your Builder shall marry you."

The link to the gospel (Matt 1:1-25) is rather clear. Joseph knew Mary was pregnant, and he knew that he was not the father. He would be a thief to claim the child, but Joseph was a holy man who strove to please God always. God's messenger assures Joseph that keeping Mary as spouse is God's plan for him. In Matthew's genealogy, the four women who appear are non-Israelites and some are of dubious character yet each won a place in God's plan. These women possess "acquired honor," thus making Jesus completely honorable since his ancestors in his genealogy possess both ascribed and acquired honor.

Responsorial Psalm: 89:4-5, 16-17, 27, 29

We return again to other verses from this lament. The refrain in particular is a most appropriate response to Third Isaiah's insight. Mention of God's "countenance" brings to mind not only the Temple where Israel went "to see" God but also Moses' experience at Mount Sinai, and other instances which made God's presence very palpable in the mighty deeds God worked for the chosen people. The final verse repeats a familiar adoption-formula often sung at the coronation of new kings (see Psalm 2). Indeed, God will remain loyal to this son-king forever; the covenant with him will remain unshaken.

* Nativity: Midnight Mass
Isaiah 9:1-6

Earlier in the book of Isaiah, the prophet's oracle was look-ing for a successor to Ahaz in whom God's promise of a last-ing destiny would be realized (Isa 7:14-15). In this chapter, Isaiah describes that successor (possibly Hezekiah, ca. 716 B.C.E.) who ascended to the throne upon his father's death. The first four verses today express hope for deliverance of the northern kingdom. The words "yoke," "pole," and "rod" refer to Assyrian domination even before 721 B.C.E. and hopes that YHWH would deliver Israel from them. It is difficult for some-one who has never lived under an occupying military power to appreciate how conquered people yearn for independence. Anyone who could deliver a nation from such a condition would be a welcome leader.

Verses 5-6 are a triumphant coronation hymn composed by Isaiah for Hezekiah, the son of God's promise in Isaiah 7:14. Wonder-counselor means this king will not need advisers such as those who led his father astray. God-Hero is a mighty warrior designation. Father-Forever describes the quality of his rule, and peace results because of the king's abilities, be-cause God promised it, and because judgment and justice now sustain the dynasty. When Hezekiah did not meet the expectations expressed in these verses and in the previous oracle (7:10-17), Isaiah projected his hopes to a later time (11:1-9). This evening's gospel (Luke 2:1-14) identifies Jesus as the one who fulfills these hopes magnificently: he is Mes-siah and Lord.

Responsorial Psalm: 96:1-2, 2-3, 11-12, 13

This is an enthronement psalm that honors God as Israel's king. Today's verses are selected from the first call to praise (vv. 1-3) and the second set of reasons given for this praise (vv. 10-13). The author of this psalm has borrowed heavily from other composers (Psalms 33; 91; 98; and Isa 42:10). The word "announce" (his salvation) is a Hebrew word from which the English word "gospel" derives. This psalmist's inspiration prompts him to broaden the vision of Second Isaiah to a more universal sweep than Isaiah imagined: The Lord shall rule not just Israel, but all the earth.

* Nativity: Mass at Dawn
Isaiah 62:11-12

Third Isaiah seeks to prevent two unfortunate choices in post-exilic Jerusalem: that the people will lose hope and settle for less than God has promised, or that they will keep high hopes and become frustrated. These concluding verses of a section proclaiming salvation for a glorious new daughter Zion (Isa 60:1–62:12) string together three uplifting titles: holy people, redeemed of the LORD, and "frequented," that is, a city that is not forgotten but rather visited by its Savior and recognized by all nations. In the accompanying gospel (Luke 2:15-20), after visiting Joseph, Mary, and the infant, the shepherds announce all that had been told to them about Jesus. Third Isaiah's vision for Zion is realized in the birth of Jesus.

Responsorial Psalm 97:1, 6, 11-12

Another post-exilic psalm which honors God as king draws also on other psalms (18; 50; 77) and Second Isaiah. The focus of this psalm and the verses selected for today is justice, which in the world of our ancestors in the faith was operative in the realm of patronage, a feature of fictive kinship. A patron is one with surplus who treats clients (needy people) as if they were family, hence, with favoritism. This is how the Lord treats his people (the just, the upright of heart), and all the people will witness this honorable behavior (his glory). The birth of a savior is a gift beyond expectation. Truly such a patron outshines all others, as the refrain reminds us.

* Nativity: Mass during the Day
Isaiah 52:7-10

Exile is a painful experience. The Polish experience is expressed in the poignant phrase *żyć na wygnaniu*, "to live somewhere after one was chased out, driven out, banished, expatriated, without rights." The notion involves a sense of belonging and security which is shattered by forced ejection from a sacred place. Without diminishing the historical and cultural uniqueness of each case, perhaps only a person who has experienced an exile can appreciate its reversal.

Today Second Isaiah reports the joy of reversal of the Babylonian exile, but from a strange perspective. It is the watchmen, the ones who did not go into exile, who shout for joy. Scholars note that it was only the elite, the intelligentsia as it were, who were taken away. Ordinary folk remained. Yet both suffered. "How can we sing a song of the LORD in a foreign land?" asked the deportees (Ps 137:4). Those who did not go into exile had no visionary leaders to lift their spirits or stir their hopes. The best news of all in the prophet's statement is that at last "all the ends of the earth" will see that God is worth believing in. God does care for and remember the people of divine concern. As this reading tells that the people saw God's redemption in progress, the gospel reading for today (John 1:1-18) speaks of Jesus as Word and light giving people the ability to see a new moment in God's redemptive will.

Responsorial Psalm 98:1, 2-3, 5-6

Today's verses drawn from yet another psalm acclaiming God as king of the universe highlight a worldwide participa-

14

tion in the reign of God. Israel is saved, all the nations are witnesses, and the entire physical universe is transformed. Because the psalm borrows from the first reading ("all the ends of the earth," Ps 98:3; Isa 52:10), it is perfectly suited as a bridge to the gospel and as a link between all the cosmic references in the readings.

Sunday within the Octave of Christmas: The Holy Family of Jesus, Mary, and Joseph
Sirach 3:2-6, 12-14

While today's gospel (Matt 2:13-15, 19-23) highlights Joseph as a responsible husband and father, this first reading focuses on the obligations of sons. Honoring one's father means to submit to the father's will and to remain fiercely loyal to the patriarch. Such a son pleases God who attends to the dutiful son's prayers. Whoever reveres his father will live a long life because the father will not have to kill the disobedient son as God requires (see Deut 21:18-21 about the glutton and drunkard; compare the opinion of people about Jesus in Matt 11:18-19). If one mirror-reads the concluding verses (12-14), that is, imagines the situation that it might plausibly be addressing, one might suspect that disrespect of fathers by sons did occur, perhaps often enough to warrant composition of these verses by the sage. Consider how Jacob at the instigation of his mother Rebecca treated his aged father, Isaac (Genesis 27). The prevailing motivation given by the sage for his advice is that God hears the prayers of a dutiful and honorable son. Considering the concern God shows toward Joseph in today's gospel, it is plausible to conclude that Joseph was an honorable son who revered his own father. When faced with challenges in his own married life, Joseph turned in prayer to God who responded favorably as the gospel indicates.

Responsorial Psalm 128:1-2, 3, 4-5

This psalm highlights the blessings that come to a person who fears the Lord. The word "fear" does not describe an emotion that causes trembling, the knees to weaken, and the like. It rather describes an awareness of who God is and how one relates to God. Acknowledging that the creature is not God will gain for the creature God's blessings in labor, in the family circle, and in all of Israel. In this case, the blessings are a fertile wife and many, presumably obedient, children.

or Genesis 15:1-6; 21:1-3

This combination of readings from Genesis highlights God's faithfulness to Abraham, granting him a son under the most improbable (nearly impossible?) conditions. As is customary in the biblical tradition, God communicates with creatures in their altered states of consciousness (in this instance, a vision), and the human person is always frightened by the experience. Thus, a common element in visions is that the one appearing calms the visionary ("Fear not!") and adds a self-identification ("I am your shield"), a role God played for Abraham to whom God was not a stranger. The "word of the LORD" that comes to Abraham is the soundtrack that Abraham the visionary supplies. It is often an insight based upon or using related experiences. Abraham deeply desired one of his own progeny as heir, and the "word of the LORD" assured him this would indeed be the case. As the final verses indicate, God kept the divine promise. In the alternative gospel that may be used in Year B (Luke 2:22-40), Simeon and Anna reveal to Mary and Joseph the plans of God for Jesus. God not only effected the conception and birth of Jesus, but also had designed a purpose for his life.

Responsorial Psalm 105:1-2, 3-4, 6-7, 8-9

This psalm too derives from the circle of Second Isaiah. The refrain emphasizes the significance of the preceding readings and underscores the theme of these selected psalm verses. The Lord remembers the Lord's covenant forever. In particular, these verses highlight how God kept the divine promises to Abraham, Isaac, and Jacob. Such a reflection upon the patriarchs is unique among the psalms. It is very appropriate in bridging the first (alternate) reading with today's (alternate) gospel (Luke 2:22-40).

* January 1 Octave Day of Christmas: Solemnity of the Blessed Virgin Mary, the Mother of God
Numbers 6:22-27

Many Christians recognize these verses as the Blessing of St. Francis written by him for Brother Leo who requested a special, personal benediction. Others may recall that these verses form the traditional conclusion to the Synagogue Sabbath service. In the context of the Hebrew Bible, these verses emphasize the "face" of God and hearken back to the experience of Moses himself: "The LORD used to speak to Moses face to face, as one man speaks to another" (Exod 33:11). In this respect Moses was considered to be unique among all the prophets: "Since then no prophet has arisen in Israel like Moses, whom the LORD knew face to face" (Deut 34:10). But what of the persistent biblical tradition that no human being could survive such a face to face encounter with God; "But my face you cannot see, for no man sees me and still lives" (Exod 33:20)? The text does not say that such a vision is impossible, only that it can be fatal. That is why people who survive can express only awe and wonder. "I have seen God face to face . . . yet my life has been spared," marveled Jacob (Gen 32:31).

In Israel, the verses from Numbers had been used as a priestly blessing from very early times during the three feasts

(Passover, Pentecost, Tabernacles) when Israelites went to present themselves to the Lord to "see his face." Thus the phrase meant going on pilgrimage to the Temple in Jerusalem. The priestly verses, then, expressed the confident hope that those who came to experience God in the Temple would not be disappointed. The gospel (Luke 2:16-21) reports the responses of some who had met Jesus face to face: the shepherds went and told others; Mary pondered these things in her heart. How would you respond to a face to face meeting with God or the Risen Jesus?

Responsorial Psalm 67:2-3, 5, 6, 8

Originally this psalm may have been a non-Israelite thanksgiving after a bountiful harvest. Appending the priestly prayer in the opening verses would have accommodated it to the Israelite tradition. When God displays the divine "face" (= self), God manifests personal delight and gracious generosity. This is God's way of dealing with human beings (vv. 2-3). Nations should rejoice (vv. 5, 6), and so should all the earth (v. 8). God deals with human beings justly, as a father deals with family members. The final verse "all the ends of the earth" (which has yielded its increase) is a fitting reference to Mary, since Jesus, the fruit of her womb, is part of this earth's "yield" (see Gal 4:4 which is the second reading for today; relate also to today's gospel). These psalm verses make a fitting bridge between all three readings.

* Second Sunday after Christmas
Sirach 24:1-2, 8-12

Known as the "Praise of Wisdom," this poem (24:1-33) begins the second major division of Sirach (24–50). Today's verses are drawn from a twenty-two-line speech delivered by Wisdom in the first person (vv. 3-17, 19-22). The author introduces Wisdom in verses 1 and 2. By themselves, these verses do indeed indicate the honorable status of Wisdom, but both to modern and especially ancient ears, they are incomplete without verse 3. Modern listeners might repeat the folk-adage, "self-praise stinks." Ancient Mediterranean listeners would bristle to hear someone speak without humility, that is, without deliberately putting oneself down a notch or two so that others can raise one up to one's proper status. Verse 3 explains why the first two verses are culturally appropriate: Wisdom came from the mouth of the Most High. This explains the respect and reputation she enjoys in the assembly of the Most High, in the midst of her people, and in the multitude of the chosen.

Twenty-two lines imitate an acrostic poem, that is, one in which each line begins with a successive letter of the Hebrew alphabet. This speech is not an acrostic. The final verses of today's reading (8-12) tell us that God commanded Wisdom to dwell in Israel because she was unable to find a suitable place elsewhere on earth by a personal search. Dwelling in the "tent" is an allusion to the dwelling that God commanded Moses to build (Exod 25:8-19; 26:1-37). That she ministers there suggests that Wisdom as Law laid down the liturgical rules to be followed in the worship of the Lord. She continued when the Temple replaced the tent, and she remains ever present among God's people. Reference to Wisdom (spoken by God) living in a tent (24:8) links nicely with the statement in today's gospel that "God's word became human and [literally in Greek] pitched its tent among us" (John 1:14).

Responsorial Psalm 147:12-13, 14-15, 19-20

These verses are drawn from the three quasi-independent hymns that constitute this psalm: verses 1-6, 7-11, and 12-20, which focus on God as Lord of Zion through the creative word. Mention of Zion and repetition of various synonyms for "word" (command, statutes, ordinances) demonstrate how these verses serve as a suitable bridge between the first reading and the gospel. Indeed, the refrain makes that explicit: "The Word of God became man and lived among us."

* January 6: Epiphany
Isaiah 60:1-6

Third Isaiah speaks a word of encouragement to the residents of Jerusalem. To offset the discouragement deriving from the trickle of returnees from exile, the prophet uses the "prophetic perfect" tense (v. 1: light has come, glory shines [has shone]), which firmly declares that salvation is still to come. An action initiated in the past is yet to be completed. Paltry beginnings should not discourage anyone. God lights up the Holy City, which invites all to gather and come (vv. 1-3). The imagery stirs hope. First the scattered deportees of Israel return ("your sons . . . and your daughters"). Then come the non-Israelites from far away. "Riches of the sea" would indicate the region north to Tyre and Phoenicia; "Midian and Ephah" point to the region south to the Arabian desert and east to the Gulf of Aqabah; "Sheba" refers to south Arabia. Some scholars think Matthew in today's gospel (2:1-12) drew inspiration from these verses of Isaiah when he mentions gold and frankincense. The passage has long been associated with the feast of the Epiphany in the liturgy.

Responsorial Psalm 72:1-2, 7-8, 10-11, 12-13

Traces of Isaiah 9:2-7 and 11:1-9 in this psalm support the opinion that it was composed in honor of King Hezekiah (715–687 B.C.E.), with verse 10 added still later (cf. Isa 60:6-10). Today's verses praise the ideal kin-person's justice and judgment (1-2). He shall establish peace over the ideal expanse of Israel: from the Red Sea to the Mediterranean, from the desert to the Euphrates ("sea to sea," vv. 7-8). The psalmist pushes the boundaries even to Spain (Tarshish) and Ethiopia (Seba, vv. 10-11)! Why should this king's empire extend so far? Because he will vindicate the lowly, poor, and afflicted (vv. 12-13). Yes, as the refrain indicates, every nation can admire such a ruler.

* Baptism of the Lord
(First Sunday in Ordinary Time)
Isaiah 42:1-4, 6-7

These verses are commonly identified as one of the four "Servant" Songs in Isaiah (42:1-4; 49:1-6; 50:4-9a; 52:13–53:12). Current scholarship suggests that they were an integral part of Second Isaiah (40–55) from the beginning and were not later additions. The Servant is Israel presented as a collectivistic individual. At the present time, approximately 80 percent of the world's population are collectivistic individuals. Such people stand in sharp contrast to individuals as they are known in Western cultures (representing just 20 percent of the world's population). Collectivistic personalities draw their identity from the group (nation, family) and do not want to stand out from the crowd. While earlier biblical scholarship talked about corporate personality, it is more appropriate today to speak of collectivistic personalities. Thus, while these Servant Songs in Isaiah sound as if they are describing a specific individual, they really describe the nation. Any individual member of this nation would readily identify with the description.

These particular verses deal with the destiny of the Servant. Above all, the Servant will reveal and establish justice or God's law to all the nations. The Servant will teach everything that is needed for leading a well-ordered life pleasing to God. Israel will not assume the posture of an arrogant and rushing victor but will rather offer a living example of obedience to God's will. In this way will she be a light to the nations. One basic link between this reading and the gospel (Matt 3:13-17) is the notion of someone with whom God is pleased: the Servant and Jesus. What kind of job description would you write for such a person?

Responsorial Psalm 29:1-2, 3-4, 3, 9-10

This hymn was borrowed from Canaanite culture where it was sung in honor of Baal, god of thunder and conqueror of the mighty waters. The Israelites substituted "voice of the LORD" for "voice of Baal" and repeated it seven times while singing this hymn in the liturgical assembly. Of course, thunder is the voice of the Lord, and these psalm verses point to today's gospel reading in which the sky is torn open and the voice from the sky says of Jesus: "This is my beloved Son, with whom I am well pleased."

or Isaiah 55:1-11 (alternate readings for Year B)

This is the final chapter of the Book of Consolation or of Comfort, as Second Isaiah is sometimes known (40–55). It blends together nearly every major theme that has occurred in this book. Moreover, it repeats many key words and themes of chapter 40 thus forming an *inclusio* with it. (An *inclusio* is a literary device whereby an author indicates that the verses or chapters contained within the *inclusio* are intended to constitute a unity.) The phrase "seek the Lord" customarily invited people to the Temple. Here Second Isaiah exhorts the listeners to find the Lord elsewhere, away from the sanctuary. God is near. The word sent by God doesn't just dangle in the air but is rather like rain that falls and permeates all creation, producing growth that points back to God. God's word, too, is effective, more like an event than a message. For the Prophet, God's word calls Israel back to her homeland which God will change into a new paradise for them.

Responsorial Psalm: Isaiah 12:2-3, 4bcd, 5-6

These verses contain two hymns of praise which may have served as a choral refrain when Isaiah was read in liturgical celebrations in the synagogue. Scholars hypothesize that the first reading was from the Torah which had been divided into 150 sections equaling the total number of Sabbaths in three years. Thus the entire Torah was read over a period of three lunar years. The second reading, called the Haphtorah, was selected from the Prophets. It may well be that a Psalm was the third reading, hence the 150 psalms.

The first hymn (vv. 1-3) quotes Exodus 15:2, which thanks God for leading the people out of bondage in Egypt. It thanks God for pardoning the people's sins. The second hymn (vv. 4-6) exhorts the people to broadcast God's honor throughout all the earth. The refrain ("You will draw water joyfully from the springs of salvation") links the water imagery in both the first reading and in the gospel (Mark 1:7-11).

Second Sunday in Ordinary Time
1 Samuel 3:3b-10, 19

The event described in these verses is identified in verse 1 (omitted from today's reading): "the word of the LORD was rare in those days; there was no frequent vision." Modern psychological anthropologists identify vision as an altered state of consciousness, one of twenty different states which human beings are capable of experiencing. It is interesting that in this "vision," Samuel doesn't seem to "see" anything. Instead, he hears the Lord and receives a message from the Lord. Today's verses also do not tell us that the message was not good news for Eli and his sons. Very likely the architects of the lectionary have carved these verses from their context to emphasize the need for openness to hearing God's word: "Speak, LORD, for your servant is listening."

Contemporary studies of altered states of consciousness add further insight. Notice that Samuel did not recognize the one speaking to him because he "was not familiar with the LORD, because the LORD had not revealed anything to him as yet." This was either Samuel's first experience of a vision, an altered state of consciousness, or it was the first time he encountered the LORD in a vision or altered state of consciousness. Very often the visionary is confused at first or doesn't recognize the one speaking until that person identifies or "reveals" self. "Fear not, it is I" is typical. Once Eli realizes what is happening to Samuel, he tells Samuel who it might be: the Lord.

It is also important not to distinguish too rigidly between what is seen and what is heard. The total experience is a unit, both elements are present. Typically, however, the visionary provides the "sound track" from the visionary's knowledge. Even if visuals are lacking, as they seem to be in Samuel's "vision," he is aware of being in an altered state of consciousness. He is also aware of being in the presence of the Lord, and the Lord communicates with him. The Lord speaks, and Samuel listens.

Such experiences are common among more than 90 percent of the world's population. Those who do not have such experiences are the ones who need to explain why. Perhaps very wisely have the architects of the lectionary selected these verses so that modern believers might pray: "Speak LORD, for your servant is listening. Help me to hear, O Lord!"

Responsorial Psalm 40:2, 4, 7-8, 8-9, 10

The phrase "I have waited" most often implies that a sad time period is almost ended (this psalm is dated between the destruction of the Temple in 587 B.C.E. and its reconstruction in 520 B.C.E.). The verses selected for today's response to the first reading underscore the importance of faith (= loyalty) and obedience. "Open ears" (literally "ears that you have dug for me") reflects a practice described in Exodus 21:5-6. A slave who was set free but elected to stay with his master had his earlobe pierced at the temple. The psalmist modifies the idea to represent an obedient listening to God's will (see also Isa 50:4-5). These sentiments form a suitable bridge between the story of the young Samuel in the first reading and the call of the first disciples in the gospel (John 1:35-42).

Third Sunday in Ordinary Time
Jonah 3:1-5, 10

After a brief sermon by the prophet, all the people have a change of heart and turn from their evil ways within a single day! The concluding verse (10) is very likely inspired by Jeremiah 18:7-8, which points out that the deity can indeed change plans if God's creatures have a change of heart and turn away from evil. Today's verses do not mention Jonah's disappointment with his success. He felt certain that his audience would not listen and would merit punishment from God. Jonah would prefer a predictable God to a God of surprises. The Hebrew name *yonah* means dove or homing-pigeon. It may have symbolized Israel's intent to limit God's mercy to herself. The experience of the prophet and the message of his book is a clear challenge to such an outlook so pointedly manifest in the prophet's response to his successful evangelization.

Responsorial Psalm 25:4-5, 6-7, 8-9

In this acrostic poem (each line begins with a successive letter of the twenty-two character Hebrew alphabet), a sinner whose enemies are exploiting his faults with a vengeance prays that God will teach him the "right way." In the entire psalm, the name YHWH is repeated ten times. There are also ten references to the Lord's way. The word "teach" is repeated three times. This psalmist is not only a clever author but demonstrates sincerity, openness, and a noble character in his determination to improve his life. Once again, the psalm links the theme of the first reading and the gospel (Mark 1:14-20) very well: repentance and an eagerness to learn the way of the Lord.

Fourth Sunday in Ordinary Time
Deuteronomy 18:15-20

A prophet is a spokesperson for God who declares God's will for the here-and-now. These verses (very likely exilic) describe the authentic prophet. A true prophet is called by YHWH, is a native Israelite, and stands in continuity with the distinctive prophetic role of Moses (see Exod 33:11; Num 12:1-8). The Israelites requested a mediator/prophet (see Deut 5:23-28) because direct interaction with God was a frightening experience for them. God promises to raise up such a mediator/prophet as the occasion requires. Only such a one, however, is authorized to speak in God's name. For this reason, listeners will be held accountable for the prophetic message. On the other hand, non-Yahwistic prophets or anyone not commissioned by YHWH (see Jer 23:9-32) will be subject to death. This reading is intended to illuminate the gospel in which Jesus is described as one who teaches with authority (Mark 1:27).

Responsorial Psalm 95:1-2, 6-7, 7-9

This psalm originated as a processional or entrance hymn as pilgrims moved toward and entered the Temple area. They would see the "rock" upon which the altar of sacrifice was located. It was not difficult to apply this image to YHWH who, in the psalms, is often acclaimed as "rock" (Pss 18:2; 78:35; 89:26). The repetition of "today" reflects a concern that is common in Deuteronomy (4:30; 5:3; 6:1; 7:11, etc.). The pilgrims making the procession would be encouraged to praise the Lord (vv. 1-2). Once within the sanctuary at the Holy of Holies, they would be exhorted to adore and praise God (vv. 6-7). Then, a reading and homily would be offered (see Neh 8:4, 6, 8, 9-12 for a sample of what they might have heard). Finally, the service would end with a warning to take to heart what had been heard. Though the pilgrims are in the presence of the Lord, they are advised to remain obedient and not harden their hearts.

Fifth Sunday in Ordinary Time
Job 7:1-4, 6-7

Today's gospel (Mark 1:29-39) describes Jesus' successful healing efforts on behalf of all who suffer a wide variety of human ills. The selection from Job does not describe an illness but rather offers Job's complaints about his predicament, a situation in which he receives little useful help or advice from his so-called friends! No one helps Job like Jesus helped those in need. Today's verses are Job's reply to Eliphaz's statement in Job 4:7, a prelude to his address to God which becomes explicit in verse 12 but begins in verse 7, when Job asks God to remember the human condition.

Here Job protests that his life is a complete misery, without any meaning now since experiencing the losses God has caused him (Job 1–2). He compares his life with three common frustrating experiences in the ancient world: forced military service, the work of a day laborer, and simple slavery. In Roman times and perhaps earlier, it was customary for soldiers to force nonsoldiers to carry their equipment. To paraphrase Jesus, "if a soldier makes you carry his equipment for one mile, go two" (Matt 5:41). Day-laborers were usually people who lost family property and therefore had to rely on the graces of someone to hire them, day after day. In the Mediterranean world, it is inappropriate to ask for a job. One has to be invited to work, and one can only hope the employer will choose you from among all those who are waiting for the invitation (see Matt 20:1-16). Finally, while slavery in antiquity had nothing in common with slavery known in the New World, for some it did involve heavy labor often during the hottest time of day in the Mediterranean. Job's conclusion? I shall not see happiness again.

Responsorial Psalm 147:1-2, 3-4, 5-6

Yhwh is the healer of Israel in this period of rebuilding Jerusalem after its destruction (587 B.C.E.). That God numbers the stars and calls each by name means that God controls the seasons of the year, notably the rainy season that is so important in this part of the world which knows only two seasons: dry (summer, the end of April to beginning of October) and wet (winter, October through April). The theme of healing, or restoring meaning to broken and disrupted lives, in this psalm makes it a fitting bridge between the first reading and the gospel.

Sixth Sunday in Ordinary Time
Leviticus 13:1-2, 44-46

At first glance, leprosy is the topic that links the gospel (Mark 1:40-45) and first reading today. These verses from Leviticus state that the priest may "certify" authentic leprosy. Once this is done, the afflicted person is declared unclean. Such a person must dwell outside the camp. Straightforward as the reading appears, there is a major difficulty. Leprosy as we know and understand it (Hansen's disease) first came to the Middle East with Alexander's armies in the fourth century B.C.E. Leviticus reflects a much earlier period of history.

What is Leviticus 13–14 talking about? Very likely it is not Hansen's disease. Rather, it is some kind of repulsive scaly condition that affected people, clothes, and walls. Why the concern? Why would God care? The "holiness and purity codes" of Leviticus can be dated to the exilic and post-exilic era. When the Babylonian captivity had ended, Ezra the priest discerned that the reason for Israel's exile was its failure to keep itself pure and holy, mainly by marrying people who were not members of the House of Israel. To assure success to Israel's fresh start after the Exile, Ezra determined that all mixed marriages should be broken up and the purity of the nation restored (Ezra 9–10).

The legislation contained in Leviticus 11–16 also dates from this period. The disparate subjects of these chapters (food, childbirth, leprosy, involuntary genital discharges) all pertain to "body openings" and "the boundary of the body." The concern centers upon what can properly enter or exit the body and upon body openings both normal, like the mouth, and irregular, like scabs on the skin.

Social scientists note that rules about social boundaries and rules about body boundaries replicate one another. Thus, a concern for purity of the social body (avoid contamination with foreigners through marriage) is reflected in a concern for purity of the physical body (foods, leprosy, discharges). Both rules reinforce the major concern: keeping the community pure. "Be holy, for I, the LORD, your God, am holy" (Lev 19:2).

The message of today's first reading is that purity of the community must be preserved at all costs. Anyone afflicted with the repulsive skin condition that causes irregular "body openings" is a risk and must be "excommunicated," especially in relation to the worshiping community. If a person had the visible condition described here, such a person was not "holy as the Lord your God is holy." The condition was not considered contagious (in fact, even real leprosy is minimally contagious), but rather polluting. Experience indicated that those who touched these afflicted people often did not contract their physical condition. They did, however, become unclean, impure, unholy just like the afflicted person. Notice the operative word both in this reading and in the gospel: "unclean." The consequence of contracting an unclean condition was that one had to "dwell apart . . . outside the camp."

For Western individualists, the impact of such a fate is difficult to appreciate. A quarantined and isolated individualist would simply take along magazines, books, CDs, a palm pilot, and computer games and patiently wait until the condition changed. Individualists don't need the company of others to find happiness and fulfillment. Yet individualists constitute only 20 percent of the current world population. Fully 80 percent of the people on the face of the planet are collectivistic personalities. Such persons depend on community for meaning in life. To expel such a person from community is equivalent to a death sentence. Leviticus is simply content to identify the problem and prescribe the action necessary for maintaining the community in holiness that it might be pleasing to God. It is Jesus who by touching such afflicted persons demonstrates that they are not polluting, they are not displeasing to God, and they should be restored forthwith to community life.

Responsorial Psalm 32:1-2, 5, 11

This post-exilic psalm of thanksgiving is the second of a group of seven identified as penitential psalms. A pious Israelite notes that God initiates forgiveness (1-2). The challenge to the sinner is to be honest and stop dissimulating (5). The experience of being forgiven or cleansed is definitely refreshing (11). Trust in the Lord!

Seventh Sunday in Ordinary Time
Isaiah 43:18-19, 21-22, 24b-25

It is probable that the notion of forgiveness of sins links this reading with the gospel (Mark 2:1-12). Immediately prior to these verses in Isaiah, the prophet recalls the great titles of YHWH: Redeemer committed to helping kin; Holy One source of all holiness; Creator of all things from nothing; King who protects his people; a new Moses; First and Last. In today's verses the prophet says that great as all these deeds were, God is about to do something far greater than anything before. God will create a new paradise far surpassing the Garden in Genesis 2. Verses 22-28 contain elements of a trial. God makes accusations against the people ("you did not call upon me") but follows this with forgiveness ("I wipe out your offenses"). This good news finds fulfillment in the ministry of Jesus reported by Mark.

Responsorial Psalm 41:2-3, 4-5, 13-14

The heart of this psalm is the petition for healing in verse 4: though I am a sinner, please heal me, O Lord. The petition is rooted in solid confidence that God will not neglect the needy among the chosen people. Despite experience which often suggests that God has indeed abandoned faithful servants to the machinations of their enemies, this psalmist is confident it will not happen to him. The conclusion indicates that it didn't.

This is the last psalm in the First Book of the Psalter (there are five, perhaps imitating the five books of Moses). The final verse of today's response concludes this First Book. The actual ending of the psalm is the preceding verse. "Let me stand before you forever" is inspired by the psalmist's participation in the Temple liturgy. Having been rescued by God from his predicament, the psalmist would willingly remain in the presence of God, safe from his enemies, forever.

Eighth Sunday in Ordinary Time
Hosea 2:16b, 17b, 21-22

The question of fasting in today's gospel (Mark 2:18-22) is a plausible basis for selecting this segment of Hosea as its partner. Fasting, or refusing to eat, is essentially a protest pattern intended to move another person to a response. Therefore fasting is a strategy that belongs primarily to the realm of politics, the realm of power. While Jesus, the broker, is among his disciples, the clients, they have a powerful mediator with God, the patron. They need no other strategy to contact and have an impact upon God. When the mediator is no longer present they can resort to fasting, an alternate means of motivating God to act on their behalf.

These verses from Hosea describe the covenant between Israel and YHWH in terms of a marriage contract. The preposition "in" that follows the word "espouse" designates what follows as the bride-price (Heb. *mohar*), the gift the groom's family offers to the bride's family. In other words, YHWH the groom is bestowing on the bride's family (and therefore on her, too) basic dispositions: justice, which is the concrete working out of right, and mercy (an attitude of giving-in-to the other), which characterizes steadfast-loving kindness (Heb: *hesed*). Thus, YHWH manifests to Israel those qualities which please the deity. If believers adopt and practice these qualities (Hosea's message) then believers won't need to resort to other strategies for moving God to a desired response (Jesus' point about fasting in today's gospel).

Responsorial Psalm 103:1-2, 3-4, 8, 10, 12-13

A psalmist very likely around 450 B.C.E., in the post-exilic age, has regained health and meaning in life (vv. 3-4) and sings gratefully about YHWH who has worked this great favor in his life. YHWH is merciful and gracious but particularly to "those who fear him," that is, who recognize their dependent relationship with God.

Ninth Sunday in Ordinary Time
Deuteronomy 5:12-15

Clearly the Sabbath links this reading with today's gospel (Mark 2:23–3:6). The match is well made. The version of the Decalogue in Deuteronomy (5:6-21) is slightly different from that in Exodus 20:1-17. This is also true regarding the command of Sabbath rest. The Exodus tradition (20:8-11) points to God resting on the seventh day after creation, hence aligning itself with the P tradition. This is the reason given for keeping the Sabbath holy. In contrast, Deuteronomy doesn't mention God's Sabbath rest but rather proposes a humanitarian consideration. Let your male and female slaves rest as you rest, for you know from experience what it means to be a slave. This is why the Lord has commanded you to keep holy the Sabbath. This would seem to be the understanding of Jesus in today's gospel. If humanitarian considerations are the foundation of the commandment, then humanitarian considerations (easing hunger, restoring a sick man to wholeness) can also legitimate relaxing the commandment.

Responsorial Psalm 81:3-4, 5-6, 6-8, 10-11

This psalm and Psalms 50 and 95 are recognized as examples of liturgical preaching during feasts celebrated in the Temple. Verse 6 ("relieved his shoulder . . . hands were freed") refers to God's action of rescuing Israel from bondage and slavery in Egypt. The selected verses constitute a suitable bridge between the first reading and today's gospel which speak of rest from slavery, from labor.

Tenth Sunday in Ordinary Time
Genesis 3:9-15

Some contemporary biblical scholars offer fresh insight to this very familiar story. All have recognized a play on Hebrew words translated "naked" in Genesis 2:25 and "wise" or "subtle" in Genesis 3:1. Polish Jesuit biblical scholar Julian Sulowski proposes this translation: "And the man and his wife were both wise (rather than naked) and did not disgrace themselves. Now the serpent was more wise than any other wild creature . . ." He believes that the sacred author (the Yahwist) is targeting Baal worship (fertility rites, sacred prostitution) with which child sacrifice was associated. The first couple were wise and did not practice sacred prostitution in the Baal cult (symbolized by the serpent). But the serpent deceived them. The conclusion of this segment (3:7) he translates thus: "And the eyes of both were opened, and they recognized that they had been shamed (or exposed, or made naked)."

Viewed in this context, today's verses (Gen 3:9-15) describe the shock and reaction of the man and the woman to what happened to them: the serpent shamed them by means of clever deception—which to this day is still a valuable strategy in circum-Mediterranean cultures for preserving one's honor, which is what the serpent successfully did: he remains the wisest of God's creatures. God punishes the serpent (which may have been a dragon that lost its legs, see Rev 12:9) and sets its offspring (other serpents) at odds with the woman's offspring (other human beings). The appropriate historico-critical, literal understanding of Genesis 3:15 is that human beings regard snakes as enemies. Father Sulowski's interpretation situates the story in the context of polemic against Baal worship.

Christian tradition, of course, has developed other interpretations of this passage. It would seem that the architects of the lectionary have dipped into later Christian tradition to link this reading from Genesis with the gospel (Mark 3:20-35) which focuses on Satan. The development of understanding of the serpent/satan from the time of the Yahwist (author of Genesis 2–3, ca. 950 B.C.E.) to Mark (ca. 69 C.E.) is too complex to consider in a homily but certainly deserving of a continuing education program (personal or communal) when opportune. Jesus is certainly not concerned about snakes but about Satan.

Responsorial Psalm 130:1-2, 3-4, 5-6, 7-8

This is the sixth of the psalms traditionally identified as "penitential" (Psalms 6; 32; 38; 51; 102; 130; and 143). It is also usually identified as an "individual psalm of lament," but given that this is a collectivistic culture populated by collectivistic (not individualistic) personalities, one needs to read the psalm more closely. Even if, as some suggest, verses 7-8 are spoken by a priest in the assembly, or are a reflection on what is occurring in the Temple liturgy, the switch from the individual in verses 1-6, to the community in verses 7-8 is typical of the behavior of a collectivistic personality. The individual finds meaning in life only in community. This being said, the psalm focuses on sin, that is, on shaming God, and is once again a suitable bridge between the first reading (the serpent shaming the first creatures) and the gospel (Jesus' enemies striving to shame Jesus).

First Sunday of Lent
Genesis 9:8-15

During Lent, the Old Testament readings present high-lights of the history of God's salvific activity on behalf of creation. In today's reading, God confirms the divine covenant with all creation: humankind and the animal kingdom. God makes three speeches (vv. 9-11, 12-16, 17) and places the rainbow in the clouds. The verses are arranged concentrically so that verses 13-16 ("my bow") are at the center. In the first speech (vv. 9-11) God introduces the topic of the covenant and highlights its central feature: the stability of the universe. Never again will God inflict such a punishment on creation. God promises that the stability and security of the universe will be permanent.

Because the Hebrew word translated as "rainbow" primarily means "bow," some scholars have suggested that God hung the war weapon on the clouds. (For the bow and arrow as God's weapon of war against Israel, see Deut 32:23, 42; Hab 3:9-11; Ps 18:14.) Contemporary scholars prefer to interpret it rather as a beautiful element of nature which God created to occur under certain circumstances (see Sir 43:11; Ezek 1:28). In selecting it as a sign for Noah, God took it as a personal reminder of this covenant and a personal reminder never again to break this peace or truce with all creation. One possible link between this reading and the gospel (Mark 1:12-15) is nature in its original status as favorable to human beings.

Responsorial Psalm 25:4-5, 6-7, 8-9

This alphabetical psalm (each verse begins with a successive letter of the Hebrew alphabet) expresses the psalmist's grateful response to God's covenant love (compassion, steadfast love, kindness, goodness, vv. 6-7) and asks God to show the "way" (throughout the psalm, and in the refrain). A fitting response to the reading from Genesis and a bridge to the gospel in which Jesus begins to proclaim the Good News of God (Mark 1:12-15).

Second Sunday of Lent
Genesis 22:1-2, 9a, 10-13, 15-18

In the Mediterranean world, young boys are raised together with the girls almost exclusively by the women. They are pampered and spoiled so that when they finally enter the men's world at the age of puberty, they have to begin to learn how to act and behave like men. To teach them this behavior, adult men apply physical discipline to the boys (see Prov 13:24; 19:18; 22:15; 23:13-14; 29:15, 17), who must learn how to bear pain and suffering without flinching or crying (see Isa 50:6; 53:7). Physical discipline is the strategy by which fathers impose their wills on their sons and teach their sons how to be loyal to the family and obedient to the patriarch. Isaac carried the wood for the sacrifice, allowed his father to tie him up, and waited obediently and in silence for the potentially deadly blow his father was about to strike. Abraham surely raised an obedient and loyal son. At the same time, apparently without applying such physical discipline to Abraham, God found the patriarch to be obedient and loyal to the divine command. Because of Abraham's loyalty and obedience, God stayed Abraham's hand and promised Abraham numerous descendants and unfailing blessing.

Responsorial Psalm 116:10, 15, 16-17, 18-19

Though the entire psalm was composed in the context of serious illness and perhaps even sentence of execution ("my bonds"), the psalmist has experienced rescue. In today's select verses, we hear the psalmist's unshaken confidence ("I believed") and his gratitude (offer sacrifice in the Temple and call upon the name of the Lord). This echoes the sentiments of Abraham and links the Old Testament reading ("your son, . . . whom you love") with the gospel ("this is my beloved Son," Mark 9:2-10).

Third Sunday of Lent
Exodus 20:1-17

This is one of two versions of the Ten Commandments in the Bible (see Deut 5:6-21). Literally in Hebrew and Greek, the "ten commandments" are the "ten words" (see Exod 34:28). The exact numbering of ten is not obvious as is evident in the different numbering by Catholics and Protestants. Moreover, critical scholars agree that although the Bible situates the origin of the commandments in the time of Moses, the present form is actually the result of a very long historical development related to Israel's institutional life, its worship, teaching, social structures. Each of the commandments has its own history, having undergone expansions by the addition of promises, explanations, reflections, and other elements. Some may even have been shortened. The present form is very likely post-exilic. In general, the commandments as we read them in today's text-segment are addressed directly by God to the people, and they are presented as a unity. They also had a consistent impact upon the life of the Israelites and are reflected in prophetic preaching (Hos 4:1-2; Jer 7:9). Echoes in the psalms (e.g., 50:16-20; 81:9-10) indicate that the commandments also played a role in Israel's worship. In the Bible, the authority of God who commands is emphasized more than the content of the individual commandments. It is a loving God who commands and who expects a response from the heart of the people chosen to receive these commandments. Thus the purpose of the commandments (or "words") is to relate the people to God. In today's gospel (John

2:13-25), Jesus is irked because some of his contemporaries involved in Temple worship appear to have lost sight of the centrality of that relationship.

Responsorial Psalm 19:8, 9, 10, 11

The verses selected from this psalm as a response to the first reading sing praise for the Torah. The psalmist has in mind all of YHWH's directives and traditions for the chosen people. God's name (YHWH) is repeated six times in our verses (LORD in small capital letters always represents YHWH in English translations), emphasizing the personal relationship that God desires to establish by means of the divine directives. This relationship "rejoices the heart" and is "sweeter . . . than syrup or honey from the comb." The refrain (from John 6:68c) transfers the reflection to Jesus' words, thus helping to establish a bridge between the Old Testament reading and today's gospel.

Fourth Sunday of Lent
2 Chronicles 36:14-16, 19-23

The Chronicler is probably a Levite cantor who manifests related concerns throughout his books. He is concerned with the aesthetic, vocal, and conservative dimensions of Temple ritual. While it may sound boring and legalistic, his work is concerned with God's word and how to please God in worship. In this final chapter, he continues to reflect upon and reinterpret the books of Kings, his source, as he explains the reason for the Babylonian Exile. In the Chronicler's view, the prophets are primarily the guardians of theocracy. They bring God's word to kings who are either blessed or judged by God according to their response. The prophetic message, so often cast in the "lawsuit pattern" (Hebrew: *rib*), made it clear that God frequently engaged in covenant lawsuit with the chosen people. In today's verses, the Chronicler clearly says it was a cumulative process of ignoring the word that provoked God's anger and brought about the Exile.

The Chronicler combines ideas from Jeremiah (25:11-12; 29:10) with notions from Leviticus (26:34-35, 43), but with a difference. While Leviticus looks to the punishment of disobedience, the Chronicler believes that an indefinitely long period (Jeremiah's seventy years) of sabbatical rests will prepare the land for the return of the exiles (see Lev 26:40-45). In other words, God will remember and remain faithful to the covenant. The report of Cyrus' decree is a fitting conclusion not only to these verses but to the entire work of the Chronicler. As John tells us in the gospel (3:14-21), God continues to rescue the chosen people, ultimately sending the Son so that everyone who believes in him may have eternal life.

Responsorial Psalm 137:1-2, 3, 4-5, 6

The annals of Sennacherib report that male and female singers were taken in the sack of Jerusalem to provide entertainment for the Assyrian court (see 2 Kgs 18:13-16). Ezra (2:41) explicitly enumerates these singers among the returnees from the Babylonian exile. The key words here are "remember" (vv. 1 and 6) and "sing." To sing the songs of Zion in unclean lands (see Amos 7:17; Hos 9:3) would be tragic. While some think this means that this psalm was sung only in Babylon, it is very probable that the returning singers would hymn it as they looked at the rubble of the destroyed Temple. A curse is laid on any Israelite who would betray or forget the Holy City. Since the left hand in the Middle East is used only for toilet functions and never for anything else, to wish that one's right hand would wither is equivalent to wishing for death. The loss of one's right hand is probably a double-death for a musician. The exhortation to "remember" is a fitting response to the first reading in which the kings obviously did not remember or heed the words of God's prophets. Both readings lead appropriately to Nicodemus in the gospel who may not have "forgotten" anything but took a long while to understand Jesus completely.

Fifth Sunday of Lent
Jeremiah 31:31-34

Having reviewed the roles of Noah, Abraham, Moses, and Cyrus in God's redemptive plan in the readings on preceding Sundays of this Lent, we turn today to Jeremiah. The younger contemporary of Jeremiah, the prophet Ezekiel, had already mentioned that God would give his people a new heart and guide them in walking according to the covenant stipulations (Ezek 36:26-27). It is Jeremiah, however, who alone in the Hebrew Bible dares to say that God will establish an entirely new covenant. Such a message is so contrary to the long-standing tradition and belief, it is no wonder Jeremiah suffered for preaching it. Such an incredible idea could only come from the source, from God. Jeremiah could not have imagined it or calculated to say it for shock effect.

Not that God would entirely reject the chosen people. On the contrary, they had strayed so far from God that God has to make a fresh start. This time around God would not rely on teachers, leaders, friends, or relatives in community, but rather upon the intimate and personal experience of each person. The key experience would be grasping God's forgiveness and mercy in restoring the people to their land. Again we notice how the individual in collectivistic cultures always manages to melt into the larger community, the collectivity.

Responsorial Psalm 51:3-4, 12-13, 14-15

The verses of this well-known lamentation for sin echo the sentiments of Ezekiel and Jeremiah very well. The psalmist realizes that it will take nothing short of a fresh creation to renovate his inner spirit. He prays for this renewal with Hebrew vocabulary drawn from the Priestly narrator of the creation story (Genesis 1). These psalm verses form a good bridge to the gospel (John 12:20-33) in which Jesus speaks of such renewals as a grain dying to produce much fruit, or a person losing life in this world to preserve it for eternal life.

* Palm Sunday of the Lord's Passion
Isaiah 50:4-7

Just like the other Servant Songs, this third in the series of four from Second Isaiah describes the nation Israel in history and in captivity. She will recognize herself in the persecuted, suffering, sick person, just as Isaiah (1:4, 6) described: "Ah, sinful nation, people laden with wickedness. . . . / From the sole of the foot to the head / there is no sound spot." The very last verses of today's text-segment are especially noteworthy. The Lord God is my help; I am not disgraced. The apparently shameful appearance and behavior of this servant is not really shameful if God is on his side. It is important for a male to defend his honor at all costs. But if a male finds himself in a losing situation such as being forced to go to court, which is a definite no-win situation, then the male's honorable behavior is to endure the worst without flinching or crying. The honorable aspect of what seems to be shameful behavior, of course, is the notion that Mark's Passion story in its entirety (Palm Sunday and Easter Vigil gospel reading together) fleshes out for Jesus. While Jesus seemed to be irredeemably shamed in the betrayal, trial, crucifixion, death, and burial in a stranger's tomb, God raised him from the dead. God must have been very pleased with Jesus to honor him in this way.

Responsorial Psalm 22:8-9, 17-18, 19-20, 23-24

This lament of a person who suffers unjustly but patiently is quoted thirteen times in the New Testament and nine times alone in the Passion story. The psalmist is not complaining, shows no bitterness, makes no allusion to sin, does not declare personal innocence, and makes no defense against unjust charges. The suffering petitioner simply places himself entirely in the hands of God. In this he finds great peace.

The first segment (vv. 8-9) reports the shameful taunts, the inhuman ridicule. The next segment literally claims that persecutors have mauled his hands and feet as would a lion (vv. 17-18). The petitioner beseeches God to hear his prayer (vv. 19-20). The final segment that announces a public thanksgiving in the assembly testifies to the fact that God came to the rescue (vv. 23-24).

The Triduum

For commentary on the Old Testament readings of the Triduum, see John J. Pilch, *The Triduum and Easter Sunday: Breaking Open the Scripture* (Collegeville: The Liturgical Press, 2000).

* Easter Sunday
Acts 10:34a, 37-43

To appreciate the readings of Easter time, it is helpful to understand a common human experience known as altered states of consciousness that are different from "normal" or "ordinary" consciousness. Brain and nervous system research indicates all human beings are capable of such experiences. Indeed, many are familiar with daydreaming, road trance (hypnosis while driving, yet obeying all laws and arriving at one's destination safely, etc.), and similar altered states. Cultures give distinctive interpretations to such experiences, but some cultures are reluctant to acknowledge them as healthy elements of human experience. Psychiatric research indicates that in some cultures, people can expect to see their deceased loved ones in an altered state of consciousness for as long as five years after the death, and sometimes longer. Anthropological studies recount that altered states of consciousness experiences are common in the circum-Mediterranean world of the present and of the past.

Peter delivers his speech within the context of his experience with Cornelius, a centurion of the Italian Cohort (Acts 10:1–11:18). In ecstatic trance, Cornelius is instructed to seek out Peter, and Peter, also in ecstatic trance, is instructed by God that all foods are clean. When Cornelius personally repeats his experience to Peter, Peter makes a speech, some verses of which have been selected for today's reading.

Of interest to our reflection is Peter's report about experiencing the Risen Jesus. Peter notes that God "granted that he be visible, not to all the people, but to us." Of course, God is the one who "hard-wired" human beings with the capacity for varieties of consciousness, and God can also select the subjects of specific experiences. Sometimes God can even communicate with "enemies" in an altered state of consciousness (e.g., Nebuchadnezzar in Daniel 2). While all human beings are indeed capable of the experience, the experiences will always be individual and culture specific.

Peter also observes that they ate and drank with the risen Jesus. This is not a literary device but rather the report of an actual experience. The Israelite tradition believed that holy men *(ṣaddiq; ḥasid)* would eat at three-legged golden tables overflowing with delicacies in "the world to come." In the Israelite tradition, the phrase "the world to come" points to that place where the righteous will go after they die and depart from "this world." Psychological anthropologists would call that world "alternate reality," in contrast to this world which is ordinary reality, or culturally "normal" reality. Thus some experiences in altered states of consciousness are experiences of alternate reality, including "the world to come" which is parallel to ordinary reality, or as the Israelite tradition calls it "this world."

Finally, Peter reports the consequences of seeing the risen Jesus in an altered state of consciousness. The apostles were commissioned to preach and testify to Jesus as appointed by God to judge the living and the dead. Anthropologists observed that two common results of alternate states of consciousness experiences are (1) the visionary finds a solution to a problem or (2) is strengthened to embark on a new path in life. Clearly Peter and the apostles experienced the second effect. This reading from Acts relates well with the gospel (John 20:1-9) in which Mary of Magdala, Simon Peter, and the other disciple find the empty tomb but do not yet experience the risen Jesus. It is the normal, first stage of experience after the death of a loved one.

Responsorial Psalm 118:1-2, 16-17, 22-23

This is an entrance psalm from a Temple liturgy, perhaps at a "Gate of Righteousness," which is offering solemn thanksgiving to God. The psalm also appears to have been associated with pilgrimages to Jerusalem on the feast of Tabernacles. It was an integral part of the Passover celebration recited in conjunction with filling the fourth cup of wine. The first two verses initiate the communal thanksgiving. Verses 16-17 echo Moses' song in Exodus 15, while the final verses (22-23) are quite likely an ancient proverb highlighting the difference that faith or loyalty can make. One person's junk becomes another person's treasure by faith. The late Fr. Carroll Stuhlmueller suggested that the psalm refrain (v. 24) "this is the day the Lord has made" is better translated "on the day when the Lord takes action." Indeed, on that day, Jesus was raised from the dead.

Second Sunday of Easter
Acts 4:32-35

Scholars recognize these verses as an ideal characterization of the community of believers. (Luke presents a glimpse of reality in 5:1-11 which may not have been a single and isolated occurrence.) Standing in contrast to Western individualism which lives by an isolating value system (each one has her or his own IRA, and his or her own plans for skilled nursing care in old age if necessary since no one wants to be a burden to his or her children, etc.), 80 percent of the world's contemporary population is collectivistic or communal in character, living according to congregating value systems. The ideal described in these verses was familiar throughout the ancient world. Aristotle said: "Friends' goods are common property" and "Brothers have all things in common" (*Nicomachean Ethics* 8.9.1-2). The Israelite tradition practiced covenant loyalty to fellow-Israelites: "There should be no one of you in need" (Deut 15:4 NAB; RSV: "there will be no poor among you"). People were reminded of their obligation to look to the welfare of fellow-Israelites: "The needy will never be lacking in the land. That is why I command you to open your hand to your poor and needy kinsman in your country: Therefore I command you, You shall open wide your hand to your brother, to the needy and to the poor, in the land" (Deut 15:11).

Of further note in this passage are the apostles' roles in managing community funds. In addition to proclamation and working mighty deeds (Acts 4:33), the apostles received donations (4:35, 37; 5:2) and redistributed them to the needy. This stood in contrast to the behavior of Temple authorities who were supposed to do the same thing but instead spent the funds on conspicuous consumption, something criticized by Jesus (see Luke 16:14; 20:45–21:4; Mark 12:38-44).

Responsorial Psalm 118:2-4, 13-15, 22-24

In this ancient psalm, the refrain and first verses (2-3) emphasize the basic reliable quality of the covenant and the God who made it. Then a specific person praises God for a welcome rescue from a difficult situation, prompting everyone to rejoice ("tents of the just"). In Acts 4:10-11, verses 22-24 of this psalm are explicitly applied to "Jesus . . . whom you crucified, whom God has raised from the dead." Once again the psalm makes a fitting bridge to the gospel (John 20:19-31), which reports another encounter of the apostles with Jesus whom God raised from the dead.

Third Sunday of Easter
Acts 3:13-15, 17-19

These verses are carved from Peter's speech after restoring a lame man to wholeness (Acts 3:11-26). Peter shames his fellow-Israelites by pointing out their key role in Jesus' death. He is blunt: "The author of life you put to death." Nevertheless, Peter notes that it was out of ignorance rather than perversity that they acted (see Luke 23:34). This can be reversed and pardoned. While it might seem as if the Israelites had thwarted God's plan, Peter notes that in the larger scheme of things God was able even through their crime to bring to fulfillment God's saving purposes announced by the prophets. Peter's closing words here exhort the listeners to turn to God (be converted) that their sins might be wiped away. As the story progresses, it seems that many in his audience were not at all shamed (Acts 4:1-3) but rather annoyed. Still, many of them believed (Acts 4:4).

Responsorial Psalm 4:2, 4, 7-8, 9

The Hebrew language of this psalm echoes all the "official" language of Temple worship. An individual, perhaps a priest or other Temple functionary, has been caught in a web of intrigue, lies, fraud, and perjury. Yet he trusts in the Lord and is not disappointed. The phrase "light of your countenance" echoes the priestly blessing (see Num 6:24-26; Ps 31:16; 80:3, 7, 9). This is an admirable and inspiring prayer of trust and confidence certainly befitting the boldness of Peter in his speech and the incredible joy of the apostles instructed by the risen Jesus in today's gospel (Luke 24:35-48).

Fourth Sunday of Easter
Acts 4:8-12

The preceding verse 7 provides important context for understanding this part of Peter's speech in the Temple after healing the man lame from birth (Acts 3:1-10). The authorities ask Peter and John: "by what power or by what name did you do this?" It is important to notice that no one in the Bible doubts the reality of the healing. The question is always about the source of power by which this happened (see Luke 20:2). In a hierarchical society such as this one, those in authority are seriously threatened by someone who has effective power to heal. And since they did not grant permission or bestow the power or authority, who did? Hence the second question: "by what name," that is, by whose authority or power are you doing this? Then Peter's answer makes complete sense: Jesus the Messiah, the Nazarene, whom YOU crucified, but whom God raised from the dead. That has to cut these authorities to the quick. This is the second time in this encounter that Peter has to explain his actions (see Acts 3:12-16), so now he adds a fresh image from the tradition about "the stone that was rejected 'by you' [words added by Peter] . . . has become the cornerstone" (Acts 4:11; Ps 118:22). The image is most appropriate in the Temple, a massive stone structure. By rejecting Jesus, the true corner stone, Temple authorities set off the collapse of the Temple's stones around them. But there is hope in Peter's final statement: "there is no salvation through anyone else." Convert while there is time!

Responsorial Psalm 118:1, 8-9, 21-23, 26, 28, 29

As the reader may have noticed, Psalm 118 is used repeatedly in the Easter season throughout the three years of the Lectionary. It is a very complex psalm because of its frequent adaptation to ceremonies at the Jerusalem Temple and its reinterpretation in the rabbinic and New Testament traditions. Originally it was part of an entrance liturgy on an occasion when the congregation would offer solemn thanksgiving to God. The phrase about the rejected stone has the sound of an ancient proverb. Perhaps it predated the psalm. In this context, however, the community acknowledges that it is the Lord who has granted rescue and victory. The final verse is a short dialogue between an individual member of the community with the entire community.

Fifth Sunday of Easter
Acts 9:26-31

It surely strained credulity among the early followers of Jesus to believe that Saul who earlier was known to be "breathing murderous threats against the disciples of the Lord" (Acts 9:1) now comes to Jerusalem to join the company of the disciples. Who would trust him? Why should they? Barnabas (whose name means "son of encouragement," Acts 4:36) took Saul under his wing and explained to the apostles that Saul "had seen the Lord and that he had spoken to him" (9:27). This experience empowered Saul to speak out boldly in the name of Jesus in Damascus.

What is noteworthy in this account is the means by which Saul is made acceptable to and trusted by the apostles: he experienced the risen Jesus in a vision, an altered state of consciousness experience, and was obviously commissioned by the risen Jesus to preach the Good News. Even though Barnabas did not learn this in a vision as Ananias had (Acts 9:10-18), Paul's sharing of the experience with Barnabas was sufficient and convincing for Barnabas, who in turn convinced the apostles. The vision is not put to any test, nor is the visionary subjected to interrogation. People accept the visionary at his word and respond accordingly.

Some, of course, do not respond favorably. The Greek-speaking members of the house of Israel, the Hellenists, sought to kill Saul, who spoke and argued with them (Acts 9:29) as Stephen did earlier (Acts 6:9). While the opponents of Stephen succeeded in killing him, Saul's opponents failed.

67

Luke contrasts Saul with Jesus, who escaped from a hostile crowd in Nazareth and fled from his home town. Saul escaped the death threats in Jerusalem and fled to his home town of Tarsus (Luke 4:28-30; Acts 9:30).

Responsorial Psalm 22:26-27, 28, 30, 31-32

These less-familiar thanksgiving verses from the well-known lament ("My God, My God, why have you forsaken me?") reflect a liturgical setting where such sentiments of peace and assurance could comfort all of God's people suffering affliction. Eventually God comes to the rescue, and the afflicted person cannot refrain from telling everyone about his good fortune. Just as Paul announced his rescue to the community, so does every one so favored by God. As Jesus notes in today's gospel (John 15:8): "By this is my Father glorified, that you bear much fruit and become my disciples."

Sixth Sunday of Easter
Acts 10:25-26, 34-35, 44-48

(Review the reflection on other segments of Acts 10 at Easter Sunday above.) Once again, as happens repeatedly in Acts of the Apostles, ecstatic trance experiences help the young community of believers in Jesus to arrive at radically new understandings. Our ancestors in the faith understood God in general under the image of a patron, who in the Mediterranean world is a person with surplus who is obligated to distribute to those in need. The patron, however, is free to select his clients and need not attend to degree of need, etc. Thus, the patron is known to treat clients "as if" they were blood relatives, that is, with favoritism and partiality. This is what Paul writes when speaking of God's "new" behavior toward non-Israelites compared with the chosen people: "As it is written, / I loved Jacob / but hated Esau" (Rom 9:13 citing Mal 1:2-3; the meaning of the sentence is not positive hate, but preference: I preferred Jacob to Esau). Only a direct message from God in an altered state of consciousness experience could work such a dramatic change in the understanding of God for Peter or anyone else in this cultural tradition (see Acts 10:9-16, 34).

In this entire Cornelius episode (Acts 10:1–11:18), a variety of people experience altered states of consciousness in which they receive communication or new understanding from God or messengers from God. In the biblical tradition, this was God's customary way of communicating with the chosen people (see 1 Sam 3:1). As Peter was speaking the Spirit fell upon the non-Israelites, who began speaking in tongues and glorifying God. Glossolalia is patterned speech and not the ability to speak foreign languages. While human beings perform glossolalia, everyone knows it is the spirit world that inspires and causes it. Thus, Peter's associates (members of the house of Israel who believe in Jesus) know that these non-Israelites are not circumcised. From this point of view, therefore, they cannot be pleasing to God. But if the Spirit chose to fall on them and gift them, how could anyone refuse them full membership into the community of those who believed in Jesus? They were baptized immediately.

Responsorial Psalm 98:1, 2-3, 3-4

This psalm acclaims YHWH as king over the universe. YHWH has acted graciously toward Israel, so it should respond with praise (in Temple liturgy, of course) in order that all the ends of the earth might witness God's rescue of the chosen people. The key gifts of God are salvation and justice or righteousness, and kindness and loyalty or faithfulness.

* The Ascension of the Lord
Acts 1:1-11

Luke alone among the New Testament authors (here and in his gospel for this day, 24:46-53) reports Jesus' ascension as an actual visible event that took place near Bethany (Gospel) on the Mount of Olives (Acts) and was observed by "witnesses," that is, the apostles. The event takes place in an altered state of consciousness; it is a trance experience. The Greek word in verse 10 (gazing intently at the sky) is the word Luke uses in Acts to identify a trance experience (see e.g., Acts 7:55, etc.).

There are two kinds of trance experiences: individual and group. This is a group type of experience (recall 1 Cor 15:6 where Jesus appeared to more than five hundred at one time). According to anthropological and psychiatric studies, it is not uncommon for those who have lost loved ones in death to have vivid experiences of them for up to five years after the event, and sometimes longer. While such experiences are especially common at the burial place, they can occur elsewhere, too.

Where do the deceased go at death? To use nontheological language, they go to alternate reality. All of reality consists of two parts: the one in which human beings presently live (called the world, ordinary reality, or culturally "normal" reality) and the one to which human beings go after they die to join God and the spirit world (called alternate reality, or in theological terms "heaven," "with God," "the world to come," and the like). Cultures who hold this understanding of reality know that there is an entryway between the two parts of reality: ordinary and alternate. It is a hole or an opening or a crack or a door between the earth and sky which a person must find in order to go from one realm to the other. According to the sacred traditions of many cultures, that hole or crack or door is located over the city in which is located the earthly abode of the deity. In Greek tradition, the hole was over Delphi. In the Israelite tradition, the hole is over Jerusalem. Thus, Jesus could not likely have ascended in Galilee (Matt 28:16), for the hole is not located there. Nor does Matthew say that. He says only that Jesus met the disciples there. Luke places the ascension at the most plausible place, where the passageway between this world and the sky is located in Israelite tradition, namely in the environs of Jerusalem. The two men in white robes are typical of Luke and are typical representative beings from alternate reality.

As one can expect in a trance experience, the apostles receive instruction from the risen Jesus just before he departs their company (stay in Jerusalem, wait for the Spirit, bear witness to the ends of the earth). The two messengers from alternate reality conclude the trance experience by promising them that Jesus will return.

Responsorial Psalm 47:2-3, 6-7, 8-9

This enthronement psalm was sung in the Temple annually at the New Year feast when the Ark of the Lord was installed anew in its place. This symbolized the Lord's definitive enthronement and was met with shouts of joy and blasts on the shofar. Non-Israelites who witnessed this event recognized the superiority of Israel's God over others. Though originating in a limited nationalistic perspective, the psalm's conclusion finds its fulfillment in the first reading and the gospel (Mark 16:15-20) for today's liturgy.

Seventh Sunday of Easter
Acts 1:15-17, 20a, 20c-26

The architects of the lectionary have omitted the verses that speak of Judas' death and concentrate instead on the selection of a successor. It is interesting to note that at least two (and perhaps more) candidates met the qualifications and were available to become "witnesses of Jesus' resurrection" (v. 22). The qualification was to have accompanied Jesus from the Baptism of John until the Ascension. Luke doesn't mention the number present at the Ascension, but it must have included more than the remaining eleven, perhaps as many as the 120 mentioned in verse 15. What is further interesting is how many are not mentioned again after this. The alternate candidate, Justus, is not mentioned again but neither is Matthias, the one selected to replace Judas. Of the eleven apostles mentioned in verse 13, nine are never mentioned again in Acts. Only Peter and John remain visible. Nor is Mary, the mother of Jesus, mentioned after this text-segment. Instead, new witnesses to the Resurrection emerge: Stephen, Philip, Barnabas, James the brother of the Lord, and Paul. While none of these individuals witnessed the actual resurrection, most (probably all) experienced the risen Jesus in altered states of consciousness experiences. This experience legitimates their testimony. Casting lots is the way God manifests the divine will to human beings (vv. 24-26).

Responsorial Psalm 103:1-2, 11-12, 19-20

Composed after the psalmist's health had revived, the verses selected for today's responsorial psalm do capture the heart of the psalm's sentiments. A key phrase (repeated three times in the entire psalm) is "those who fear him," that is, those who know who God is, who they are, and who live that relationship honestly. In the opening strophe (vv. 1-2), the word "soul" literally in Hebrew can mean "throat" (Isa 5:14; Hab 2:5) and metaphorically can designate longing, yearning, craving, desiring, earnestly striving after someone or something. The psalmist yearns with his total being after God and is grateful that God is in his life. The reason, of course, is God's steadfast loving kindness, a virtue extended only to one's kin, hence assuring this God-fearing psalmist of being part of God's family. The concluding strophe is assuring because God resides high above the sky in the constellation known as "throne" visible to those who can read the constellations of the sky. All else is beneath the throne, thus all God's minions (the hosts of heaven, the angels) are invited to bless and acknowledge God, too. If the context of today's gospel (John 17:11b-19) is the evening meal, then when Jesus raises his eyes to the sky it is because he knows where the throne is even though the meal takes place indoors.

* The Vigil of Pentecost
Genesis 11:1-9

According to the biblical account, Babylon (Babel) was the first city built by humans after the Flood. It is the first city of our era of humankind. The biblical story of Babylon further teaches that this is where humankind, which had been united at that time, became quite divided, and where diverse human languages originated. It was a punishment levied by God against the builders for their audacity. Extra-biblical traditions help us to fill in gaps in our high-context biblical reports. Nimrod, grandson of Ham son of Noah, was the first "mighty man" on earth (Gen 10:8). Relying on the Greek translation (LXX), Philo of Alexandria noted that Nimrod began to be a "giant" on earth. He wanted to take revenge against God for flooding the earth and for killing his forefathers, so he decided to build a tower higher than the water could reach, perhaps even into the sky, the realm of God (see Josephus, *Antiquities* l.113-114).

The name "Babel," in Akkadian, means the "Gate of God." Thus this city, Babylon, and its tower were intended to be the place where God and humans could meet and enter each other's territory. Since God came down to visit and look around, it seems that the technology worked (see Gen 10:8)! It is the only city in the world to which God descended to make a personal visit. But the tower which was originally intended to maintain the unity of humankind (see v. 4) begot human discord instead. The Genesis story doesn't say why, but later, extra-biblical traditions of Israel, as noted above by

Josephus, do. Nimrod's plan was set in motion in contempt of God! For this, the city would eventually be destroyed.

In Israel's history, God used this city to punish Judah. Its ruler, Nebuchadnezzar, destroyed the Temple and took the elites into Exile (see Jer 20:4). But God still intended to destroy Babylon (see Isa 14:22; 21:9). After his conquest of Persia, Alexander the Great was going to make Babylon the center of his worldwide empire, but his successors abandoned the idea and the city. By the first century A.D. Babylon was in ruins and deserted, exactly the image presented by John the Revealer (Revelation 17–20).

or Exodus 19:3-8a, 16-20b

God comes to visit humans in this reading, too. God offers to make a covenant with the Israelites. If they accept—and it is always a matter of freely accepting the offer—they will be God's special possession. They must hearken to Yhwh's voice and not to the voice of any other god. The word "possession" in Hebrew and in Akkadian has the meaning of "treasures of the wealthy and of the king." This sense of the word also occurs elsewhere in the Hebrew Bible (Deut 7:6; 14:2; 26:18; Ps 135:4). Scholars are not certain of the meaning of "kingdom of priests." Since the phrase occurs with "holy nation," it can be considered somewhat synonymous. If Israel agrees to God's offer, to be special to God, it will be set apart from others (basically, that is what holy means), sacred among nations as priests are among people.

Then God appears in verses 16-19. Like other theophanies in the Bible, this one takes place in a storm (see Exod 15:8, 10; Judg 5:4-5; Pss 18:6-19; 29; 77:16-20). The text actually mingles into the original event at Mount Sinai some elements of subsequent liturgical reenactments. For instance, the trumpet blast replicated the thunder; the furnace or fire pot replicated the smoke. This is how later generations repeated and celebrated this foundational experience with God. In the last verse, God establishes the mediating role of Moses by summoning him to the top of the mountain.

or Ezekiel 37:1-14

"I have promised, and I will do it, says the LORD" (v. 14). What comforting words spoken by the prophet. Ezekiel reports another of his many vision experiences, an altered state of consciousness experience. Verses 2-10 report the vision while verses 11-14 (these bones are the whole house of Israel) give the explanation. Interpretation is never easy or direct because the vision is usually not linear or sequential. This means that the visionary sees many images which have to be sorted out in the interpretation. Ezekiel sees a huge number of dead, dry bones. Whose bones are these? What do they mean? Is God going to restore dead people to life? The interpretation begins in verse 11 where God identifies the bones as Israel in Babylonian exile. God tells the prophet of the divine intent to bring these dead bones back to life, that is, to give new life to dead Israel. It is not at all a promise of restoring individual people to life.

Throughout this passage there is a play on the word "spirit" repeated in verses 1, 5, 6, 8, 9, 10, 14. The Hebrew word *ruah* can mean the wind, breath, spirit (of God in this context). In verses 2-8, no wind, breath, or spirit is present at all. In verses 9-10, Ezekiel is commanded to pray to "the spirit," and in verse 14 God finally declares: "I will put MY spirit in you that you may live!" Altered states of consciousness experiences lend themselves to such fluidity of interpretation.

or Joel 3:1-5

A devastating plague of locusts coupled with a drought (perhaps in the last half of the fifth century B.C.E. and the first half of the fourth century B.C.E.) are the occasion of Joel's oracle. When both these tragedies end, Joel recognizes this as a saving deed worked by YHWH. This is a sure sign that YHWH is present in the midst of Israel. One consequence of YHWH's presence is a pouring out of God's Spirit, which produces ecstatic experience (see Num 11:24-30; 1 Sam 10:10). That old men dream dreams and young men see visions may be an indication of cultural expectations concerning altered state of consciousness experiences, but not inflexibly. Moreover, there are signs in the sky that YHWH is at work rescuing Israel.

Responsorial Psalm 104:1-2, 24, 27-28, 29, 30, 35

The refrain focuses our attention on the common element in the four readings proposed for this vigil. "Lord, send out your Spirit, and renew the face of the earth." In this psalm, the poet (a very capable master of language) reflects on creation explaining why and how God the creator acts. The final strophe is particularly appropriate. YHWH is master of life and death. The psalmist observes the cycle of life, death, and new life which the Lord has established. It is evident in all of creation, even in the life of Israel. And it is all a gift bestowed by God's spirit.

* Pentecost
Acts 2:1-11

Luke reports yet another group type trance experience in which each member of the group becomes aware of being filled by a holy spirit. Belief in spirits was common in the ancient world, and a variety was recognized: good, malevolent, and capricious. The members here recognize that they are encountering a good or holy spirit. Luke mentions two elements of the trance: what is seen (visual) and what is heard (sound). The sound, a "noise like a strong driving wind," comes from the sky. This means it has an other-than-human source. The Israelite tradition considered thunder to be the sound of God's voice (Psalm 29; Mark 1:11), though people could differ in their interpretation of the sounds they heard (John 12:29). Since the word for wind can also mean spirit, the sound indeed is of a strong wind or spirit filling the entire home. The visual element, what everyone saw in this group trance, was "tongues as of fire." This would plausibly be a red color perhaps tinged with yellow. In trance, colors identify the level of the trance, from light to deep. These colors indicate a deeper trance. The tongue shape of the fire quite likely relates to the result to which the vision plausibly contributes, namely, speaking in tongues (glossolalia). But the shape of a tongue also reminds one of a slit or opening between ordinary reality and alternate reality. If this is true, then the gathered community is at stage one of the trance (seeing geometric patterns) and Luke's report may already be anticipating what the community learned in stage two (searching for meaning in what is seen) or stage three (often arriving at totally unexpected insight).

Contemporary scholars familiar with the extensive research on glossolalia note that either Luke or his source misunderstood and therefore misinterpreted the phenomenon. In glossolalia, speech becomes musical sound. It is lexically noncommunicative, that is, this is not the informative or communicative side of discourse. Messages or insights are very rare. The musicality of glossolalia is a regular series of pulses of accented and unaccented syllables, and it is learned. One can imitate what one hears even at the first instance (see 2 Sam 10:5-12), though sometimes it occurs without a model to imitate. It is also possible that Luke deliberately speaks of foreign languages in his report (Acts 2:4, 8-11) in order to present this event as a reversal of the Babel experience of the confusion of languages (Genesis 11).

Notice that the devout Judeans were divided in their assessment of the event. Some thought the speakers were drunk (see v. 13), while others believed that it was of God because they were speaking of "the mighty acts of God." As with all trance experiences, interpretation is key. In this report, the audience interprets what they hear, the speakers do not interpret what they are saying. Even in the speech he makes, Peter does not interpret what was said. He identifies the experience as an authentic trance, induced by the Spirit, and then he takes the occasion to preach about Jesus.

Responsorial Psalm 104:1, 24, 29-30, 31, 34

Some different verses are selected from the same psalm used on the Vigil of Pentecost. Again the refrain highlights the key idea: God's spirit is an agent of renewal. It is worthwhile to ask God to send forth the Spirit to renew all creation.

Trinity Sunday
Deuteronomy 4:32-34, 39-40

Peasant populations are typically focused on the present because the pressures of survival leave no leisure to imagine a future. When problems occur, the solution is always to be found in the past. Thus, this reflection on the unique vocation of Israel encourages them to seek guidance from the past ("the days of old, before your time") and from creation which bears the traces of God's will for it. Verse 34 reflects Exodus language and strengthens the bond between the uniqueness of YHWH and the unique position of Israel among all the nations of the earth. As a result of this, Israel must never forget there is but one God and must keep God's statutes and commandments. Thus, the law that Moses is about to promulgate has as its purpose to present a challenging level of moral performance that would be compatible with the self-revelation of Israel's God and Israel's high calling. Only by keeping God's covenant and obeying God's law will Israel find prosperity and long life in its land which God gives forever. No doubt the significance of pairing this reading with the gospel for today's feast (Matt 28:16-20) is to remind believers that God is one, and Trinity means not three gods but three persons in one God.

Responsorial Psalm 33:4-5, 6, 8, 18-19, 20, 22

The verses selected from this hymn of praise are drawn from that part of the hymn which gives the motivation for praising God. God loves justice and right, God is kind, God created by the power of word alone. The words of the psalmist which follow the reading from Deuteronomy remind the listener that God's breath or word expressed in Law is creative and life giving. God looks down from heaven with keen interest, unwavering steadfast love, and omnipotent protection.

Eleventh Sunday
in Ordinary Time
Ezekiel 17:22-24

These verses are quite likely selected because the mention of creatures living in the cedar tree is superficially related to Jesus' mention of birds living in the mustard bush (Mark 4:26-34). Beyond this association, however, the readings do not have anything in common. Ezekiel presents an allegory in 17:1-10 whose features relate to historical personages and places like Nebuchadnezzar, king of Babylon, Jerusalem, Johoiachin, Zedekiah, etc. Then the prophet interprets the allegory in verses 11-18 by noting that Zedekiah was wrong in breaking a covenant he had made with Nebuchadnezzar, and in verses 19-21 YHWH replaces Nebuchadnezzar as the one who will use the Babylonians as a weapon for punishing Israel. Finally, verses 22-24 return to the imagery of the opening fable. The new twig is a future Davidic king (see 2 Sam 7:13), and the trees of the field are kings of the surrounding nations who will recognize the power of YHWH. This is the God who will raise a new king from the humility of exile to which Judah has fallen as noted in the first twenty-one verses of this chapter.

Responsorial Psalm 92:2-3, 13-14, 15-16

The palm tree can live two hundred years and grows like the cedar of Lebanon, which lives still longer. This is the length of life promised to a just person well established in the house of the Lord. Palm trees were part of the Temple in Ezekiel's vision (42:16, 22), and the symbolism of strength and royal magnificence of palm trees and cedars are evident in 1 Kings 6:29; 7:2, 7; 9:11. Isaiah (9:14) uses these images to represent Israel's rulers. The psalmist notes that the longevity and green youthfulness of the just (like the palm and cedar tree) are recompense for loyalty to God. That's one reason why it is good to give thanks to the Lord.

Twelfth Sunday in Ordinary Time
Job 38:1, 8-11

The link between this reading from Job and the gospel (Mark 4:35-41) is the working of nature as God has created it. In the world of our ancestors in faith, human beings did not fully understand how nature worked nor could they control it. In the gospel, Jesus appears to have control over nature, hence he seems to know nature in a way that Job didn't.

The storm or whirlwind is a common vehicle employed by God for self-disclosure, especially to the prophets (see Isa 29:6; 40:24; 41:16; Jer 23:19; 30:23; Ezek 1:4; 13:11, 13; Zech 9:14). It swept Elijah up to the sky (2 Kgs 2:1, 11). Throughout this book, Job has been demanding that God should answer him and explain his situation. He has even appealed beyond God to some god beyond that. God's reply is a challenge to Job. "What do you know about creation?" The reply may sound like that of a bully, but it actually fits well with Job's ongoing dialogue with his three companions. They represent the Wisdom tradition in which sages were expected to think about and explore the workings of nature (see 1 Kgs 4:29-34). God's answer is that for all their reflection on nature, neither your friends nor you understand it at all. There is a rationale in nature that surpasses your comprehension.

Responsorial Psalm 107:23-24, 25-26, 28-29, 30-31

The verses selected from this psalm of thanksgiving relate to one kind of distress against which human beings in the ancient world had little power, namely dangers in travel by sea. This is curious since only for a brief period during the rule of Solomon and Jehoshaphat (1 Kgs 9:26-28; 22:49) did Israel have at its disposal a fleet of ships. They sailed from Ezion-geber in the direction of the Red Sea. Jehoshaphat's ships were wrecked even before they got under way (1 Kgs 22:59). Still, experience on the Sea of Galilee which generates sudden storms (Mark 3:35-41, today's gospel) could also stir the same sentiments as experience on a larger body of water. Those who sail cry to the Lord in their distress, and God rescues them. The Lord's love is everlasting.

Thirteenth Sunday in Ordinary Time
Wisdom 1:13-15; 2:23-24

These verses were probably selected as a companion to the account of Jesus' restoring Jairus' daughter to life (Mark 5:21-43). In their own context, however, the author of Wisdom is not talking about physical death but rather spiritual death, the state of being separated from God for all eternity (see Wis 2:24). Nothing in the physical world (e.g., "a destructive drug") can contribute to spiritual death. Justice leads to immortality, which is a free gift of life eternal with God.

Verses 23-24 are the first biblical text-segment to equate the serpent of Genesis 3 with the devil. (In later tradition, see John 8:44; Rev 12:9; 20:2.) God's plan for human beings was not innate immortality ("immortal") but rather eternal life with the deity. The devil was envious of this, and envy in the Mediterranean world always entails a wish for the destruction of the object envied. Intertestamental traditions suggest that the devil was envious that human beings were made in God's image (*Life of Adam and Eve* 12–17) or because the first human had control over all creation (2 Enoch 31:3-6). Driven by this envy, the devil brought spiritual death into the world, but it is experienced only by the wicked ("those who belong to his company").

Responsorial Psalm 30:2, 4, 5-6, 11, 12, 13

This is a thanksgiving psalm composed by a very sick person who was at the brink of death (netherworld; the pit) but rescued by God. The psalmist invites the entire congregation which has heard his story to join in his thanksgiving. He exhorts them to be loyal, for all distress is but temporary. In the end, God will rescue the one who remains faithful.

Fourteenth Sunday
in Ordinary Time
Ezekiel 2:2-5

It would seem that Ezekiel's audience (rebellious house) and Jesus' fellow villagers (Mark 6:1-6: resistant listeners) are the reason for linking these two readings. Notice that the Lord speaks with Ezekiel in the customary divine tradition, in an altered state of consciousness. This report is part of Ezekiel's call to be a prophet (Ezek 1:1–3:27). The spirit entered him and stood him upright, that is, the spirit induces an ecstatic experience in him (cf. 1 Sam 10:10). He then receives his charge to speak to a people so stubborn they not only will not listen but actively oppose him. He must speak in spite of all opposition. The last line "they shall know . . ." is Ezekiel's typical conclusion to nearly all his oracles. By this statement, he means to indicate that it is YHWH's word, not his, YHWH's doing, not his. Ezekiel is but YHWH's spokesperson, declaring God's will for the here and now. This is the essence of what it means to be a prophet.

Responsorial Psalm 123:1-2, 2, 3-4

This pilgrimage psalm was composed for a time of distress (either individual or communal). The prayer is that God would eventually heed the rest of people who place their confidence and trust in the deity. The image is the household. God is the lord of the household who dispenses all good things to everyone. Since they are dependent on the good grace and mood of the lord of the household, servants watch the lord's hands. The maid also depends upon the good graces of the mistress of the household. With this image fixed, the congregation now begs: Have pity on us, O Lord. If, as some scholars propose, this psalm dates from the Persian period, we can understand why the congregation suffers contempt and mockery. They seek rescue from God, speedy intervention.

Fifteenth Sunday in Ordinary Time
Amos 7:12-15

Quite likely this Old Testament and gospel reading (Mark 6:7-13) are intended to be related by the idea of God's spokespersons going away from their home base to preach the message in a different locale. Mark does not limit the mission of the Twelve in the way Matthew does (10:5-6). Amos is the first of the "classical prophets," that is, the first whose oracles were written down, saved, and transmitted in a "book." He was a Judahite, that is, from the south, whose prophetic career took him to Israel, the Northern Kingdom. As such, even in the house of Israel, he would be considered an outsider. The treatment he received appears to reflect this. Amaziah, the priest of Bethel, speaks to Amos in these verses spewing contempt at him. The word he uses for prophet *(hozeh)* is correctly translated in today's verses as "visionary" or "seer," but it is not the customary word for prophet *(nabi)* and somewhat obsolete. The priest may be insinuating that Amos is not what he claims to be. Further, since prophets spoke the will of God for the here and now, his message concerned the social and political corruption of the Northern Kingdom, which would eventually lead to subjugation by Assyria. The priest's advice is simple: "Get out of here, you fraud. Go back to where you came from!" Amos' response is that this mission is not his choice but God's appointment. He admits to Amaziah that he is not a *nabi,* nor did he belong to such a circle, a "professional" guild of prophets as it were, but God selected and appointed him, and prophesy is what he must do to the people Israel. God's charge ("Go, prophesy") contrasts with and negates Amaziah's ("Go, do not prophesy").

Responsorial Psalm 85:9-10, 11-12, 13-14

The Lord proclaims peace, perhaps after the fashion of Isaiah 57:19-21, a peace that will bring healing to all. This is what God is about to do. If God's people respond to the gifts of kindness and truth, justice and peace, then the soil will once again become productive. They are praying for a good agricultural year in this psalm which seems to have been used at this festival. The damage of the exile will be undone, but the people must embrace righteousness. God will respond with good autumn rains.

Sixteenth Sunday in Ordinary Time
Jeremiah 23:1-6

Jeremiah began his prophetic career as a propagandist for King Josiah's reform (622–621 B.C.E.), calling the people of Judah to repentance. When Josiah was killed in a futile attempt to head off the Egyptian army on their way across Palestine to help the weakened Assyrian army to fend off Babylon, a son who succeeded him, Jehoiakin, became an Egyptian vassal.

Jeremiah was livid. He preached against trusting in Egypt and thereby irritated King Jehoiakin, who tore up Jeremiah's dictated prophecy. Optimistic prophets rallied to the king's support and persecuted and harassed Jeremiah for his never-ending gloom-and-doom message to Judah. The verses selected for today are Jeremiah's response to the "optimistic" prophets. Recent kings have been bad shepherds whose political maneuverings have hurt the people. A righteous king will emerge soon who will be a truly worthy successor to David. God's people need to know God's will. They do not need to hear feel-good messages that make the prophet popular. God's people need courageous leaders to face reality squarely rather than to engage in deception and false optimism.

Responsorial Psalm 23:1-3, 3-4, 5-6

This psalm echoes Israel's exodus under Moses or its experience at the end of Exile. God's tender care stands out, for God is *the* shepherd whom human leaders strive to imitate.

Verses 5-6 reflect a temple liturgy of thanksgiving ("you spread the table before me") and personalize the sentiments ("The Lord is *my* shepherd").

Seventeenth Sunday in Ordinary Time
2 Kings 4:42-44

The superficial link between this reading and the gospel (John 6:1-15) is feeding a crowd with incredibly few resources. This reading from 2 Kings is the final story in a collection of four about Elisha, the man of God, who performs wonders of various kinds. He and Elijah, his master, were known as "prophets of action" (in contrast to the classical prophets who were known as "prophets of the word"). At one level, the sacred author seeks to demonstrate that Elisha was equal in power to his master, Elijah. Just as Elijah resolved a food shortage for the widow of Zarephath (1 Kgs 1:1-15), so does Elisha resolve a food shortage.

The Elisha stories follow a pattern in which a problem is presented, a tension is highlighted, and the man of God comes up with a solution. The problem is the famine (v. 38). One hundred men, very likely companions of Elisha, are hungry ("sons of the prophets," see 2 Kgs 2:7, 16, 17). Tension is introduced when an unnamed man brings twenty barley loaves and fruit from his orchard to the man of God. Since these barley loaves are "bread of the first fruits," and the famine has been going on for quite a while, we get an idea of how severe their hunger may have been at this point of the story. It has not yet been assuaged or relieved.

The number of loaves (twenty) heightens the tension. Can one hundred men be satisfied with twenty loaves of bread? The servant is skeptical, but Elisha highlights the generosity of the donor and confirms it with a word of the Lord. That word is God's immediate response to the pressing need in time of famine. Its meaning: be generous, share—and there will even be leftovers.

Responsorial Psalm 145:10-11, 15-16, 17-18

This alphabetical psalm (the first word of each verse begins with a successive letter of the Hebrew alphabet) probably dates from late in the post-exilic age. The verses selected for today highlight God's goodness and providence. All sustenance ultimately comes from God.

Eighteenth Sunday in Ordinary Time
Exodus 16:2-4, 12-15

This reading links to the gospel (John 6:24-3) with the idea of God providing nourishment (manna) for the people. The story in Exodus is one of many tests of the people's allegiance to God. The tests involve food and drink for the people, as in these verses, or Moses' authority. Other versions of this story appear in Numbers 11 and Psalms 105:40; 78:17-31. The people grumble against Moses and Aaron, but actually they are grumbling against God. Incredibly, they prefer the Pharaoh's nourishment to that which God gives them. God does not rebuke them but provides food in the form of quail and manna. The quail is a migratory bird that comes to Palestine and the Sinai in March or April following the wind. If the wind shifts, the exhausted birds land and are easy to catch. The manna is a honey-like dropping from the tamarisk tree of the same regions. These droppings are actual secretions of scale lice and cannot be harvested in great quantity. The sacred author's point is that God comes to the aid of the people with manna in a manner that is not a usual occurrence. Bedouin of the region call these droppings *mann,* the Hebrew Bible presents a folk etymology: *man hu* ("What is it?"). "It is the bread the Lord has given you to eat."

Responsorial Psalm 78:3-4, 23-24, 25, 54

Psalm 78 retells Israel's history and includes observations about God's impatience with the people and God's rebuke and punishment to the people. Those elements are omitted in the verses selected for today's response. The focus is on God feeding the people with bread from heaven, "the bread of angels." This latter phrase designates a source of superhuman strength, something the people would need in the desert. The final line ("brought them to his holy land") is God's approval of Israel's long process of acquiring the country.

Nineteenth Sunday in Ordinary Time
1 Kings 19:4-8

God's provident feeding of Elijah with a hearth cake and water links this reading to the gospel reflection on Jesus as the bread come down from heaven. The circumstances of Elijah's journey into the desert are Ahab's continuing commitment to Baal and the people's less than certain loyalty to YHWH. Elijah proceeds to Horeb, the mountain where Moses encountered God in ecstatic trance (Exod 3–4; 33:18–34:8). Elijah seeks to encounter God here too, and of course to save his life. Curiously, in his successful escape he prays for death! After a day's journey for which he seems to have taken no provision, he is fed in ecstatic trance by an angel of the Lord. The nourishment is powerful enough to sustain his journey for the next forty days and nights until he reached the mountain.

Responsorial Psalm 34:2-3, 4-5, 6-7, 8-9

These verses give thanks to God who answers prayers and provides rescue to those who request it. The phrase "angel of the Lord" is a reverential way of talking about YHWH, very much like "name of the Lord" or "face of the Lord." The reference is to the person of YHWH, and very often this "angel" merges into the person of YHWH (see Gen 16:9, 13; Exod 3:2-6). The "angel" most commonly is associated with YHWH's help in danger and in war (see Exod 23:20-33). The exhortation to "taste and see" is an invitation to learn by experience, in this case, the experience of being nourished by God.

Twentieth Sunday
in Ordinary Time
Proverbs 9:1-6

The banquet prepared by Wisdom is associated with Jesus' continuing reflections on the living bread that came down from heaven in today's gospel (John 6:51-58). Dame Wisdom has built a house with seven columns, similar to Solomon's temple which had seven columns (1 Kgs 7:17). Yet scholars are not agreed on the meaning of this structure: Is it a house, palace, or temple? Are the pillars physical or merely symbolic? Whatever interpretation one gives, the house is indeed very impressive and imposing. The food she offers (literally bread and wine, v. 5) is a common symbol in the Hebrew Bible for spiritual nourishment (see Isa 55:1-3; Sir 15:3), giving these verses an even stronger link with the gospel. The nourishment is intended for the simple, or those who lack understanding. In Proverbs (e.g., 10:13, 21), this latter phrase often describes people opposed to wisdom, folks for whom there is not much hope. Clearly Dame Wisdom does not give up on anyone. Her gift, offered throughout Proverbs 1–9 is life and "the way." Indeed, only a fool would reject these.

Responsorial Psalm 34:2-3, 4-5, 6-7

These verses are part of an invitation to the congregation to join the psalmist in thanksgiving. The psalmist is a poor one, a simple person, who was in great distress and was rescued. The psalmist is a living example for all to see: if God helps me, the lowliest of the lowly, God will surely help others. Look to God and you will not be shamed but you will radiate joy.

Twenty-First Sunday in Ordinary Time
Joshua 24:1-2a,15-17, 18b

A few things are noteworthy about Joshua's proposition. First, he calls for a definitive, once-and-for-always choice. It was common for many people in antiquity to choose gods appropriate to the moment. In contrast, Israel was faced with a more radical choice, one that would determine her future existence as well as her cult. Joshua and his family lead the way by personal example. Second, the decision here is made by the family patriarch or elder for the entire family. This reflects the normal way in which collectivistic personalities function (see also Acts 16:15, 31-33). Collectivistic personalities currently comprise 80 percent of the world's population. They stand in stark contrast to individuals or individualistic personalities. Families comprised of individualistic personalities would take a family vote, with each member free to make a personal decision. Third, no force or threat is leveled at the people. The heads of the households are free to decide for or against YHWH. Finally, whereas Joshua based his reasoning on YHWH's victories in battles, the people base their decision upon God's provident care for them and God's leading them from captivity. Their decision concurs with Joshua's. This challenge was indeed hard. "Who can accept it?" (John 6:60-69, today's gospel).

Responsorial Psalm 34:2-3, 16-17, 18-19, 20-21

Very likely written by a person who experienced more than a normal share of life's problems, this alphabetical psalm highlights thanksgiving and instruction. Today's verses emphasize a principle of moral retribution: God rewards the good and punishes the evil. God actively confronts evildoers, but their downfall is due in part to their own misdeeds. Most importantly, God watches over the just.

Twenty-Second Sunday in Ordinary Time
Deuteronomy 4:1-2, 6-8

In Deuteronomy, Moses is preeminently a teacher (Deut 1:5; 4:5; 5:31; 6:1). His teaching includes positive legal decrees (statutes) and judicial decisions based on case law (decrees, ordinances). Observance of the Law is an absolute requirement for gaining and maintaining possession of the land. If they faithfully observe this Law, Israelites will manifest to all nations their wisdom and intelligence (or discernment, which is one way of describing the wisdom tradition of other nations). This is what the Israelites should learn. The injunction not to add or subtract from the Law is probably the sentiment that links this reading with today's gospel (Mark 7:1-8, 14-15, 21-23), which concerns "the tradition of the elders," something the Pharisees added to observance of the Torah.

Responsorial Psalm 15:2-3, 3-4, 4-5

This psalm enumerates the requirements for entering the Temple precincts, or more exactly the requirements for taking part in Temple services. It could have served as an entrance rite for Temple services, as an examination of one's behavior especially regarding failures in speaking truth or using wealth to damage the innocent. Interest rates in the ancient world sometimes hovered between 33 to 50 percent. The Torah condemned taking such advantage of needy fellow Israelites (Exod 22:25; Deut 23:19). These verses reflecting some of the commandments serve as a suitable bridge between Deuteronomy and today's gospel.

Twenty-Third Sunday in Ordinary Time
Isaiah 35:4-7a

First Isaiah describes what will happen in the return from Exile, God himself will bring it about. The result will be a reversal of circumstances: the blind will see, deserts will become fertile, etc. Isaiah's ideas become clearer as the reader recognizes that the prophet has organized his thoughts according to a pattern of perception that permeates the Bible. Our ancestors in the faith viewed human beings in terms of three zones on the human body interpreted symbolically: heart-eyes (zone of emotion-fused thought); mouth-ears (zone of self-expressive speech); and hands-feet (zone of purposeful activity). They did not see the human person in three zones, but rather they evaluated human beings by attending to what was said, perceived, done, etc. They paid attention exclusively to external things, since only God could look inside a person and read hearts (1 Sam 16:7).

Thus, the blind (heart-eyes zone malfunction) will see; the deaf (mouth-ears zone malfunction) will hear; the lame (hands-feet zone malfunction) will leap; the mute (mouth-ears zone malfunction) will sing. God restores human beings to wholeness and integrity. God also vivifies "dead" parts of creation. In the gospel (Mark 7:31-37), Jesus restores health to a man's mouth-ears symbolic body zone, and the man and the crowd proceed to announce the Good News to all.

Responsorial Psalm 146:7, 8-9, 9-10

Today's verses are drawn from the first in a series of "Hallel" or "Praise" psalms. They underscore the fact that all salvation, all rescue, all healing, all meaning in life come from God alone. In these verses, the psalmist is especially concerned with the hungry, those in prison, the blind, those who are oppressed, those whom illnesses may have brought low, the resident aliens, the widows and orphans. It is very likely that the psalmist himself is in one of these categories. Yet he is confident that God will thwart the wicked, those who cause these problems. May this God reign forever in the hearts of faithful believers, to which the congregation replied: Alleluia!

Twenty-Fourth Sunday in Ordinary Time
Isaiah 50:4c-9a

It is well to remember the core values of Mediterranean culture when reading these verses from the third of Isaiah's four Servant Songs: honor and shame. Honor is a claim to value and an acknowledgment of that claim; shame is a denial of the claim or a failure to negate the denial. In these verses, insults ("beat me," "plucked my beard," and "buffets and spitting") are a very clear indication that other citizens are not granting the Servant's claim to worth or value. In this cultural context, the Servant has to be judged a cultural failure. This is why the key statement in today's reading is verse 7: "The Lord GOD is my help, / therefore I am not disgraced; . . . I shall not be put to shame." The Servant himself is firmly convinced that God has indeed called him, opened his ears to hear, inspired him to speak truthfully. Even though his pronouncements have brought him abuse, rejection, and shame instead of respect and acclaim, God will vindicate him and restore honor to him. "Who will prove me wrong?" is the Servant's challenging question to his opponents. In the gospel (Mark 8:27-35), Jesus expects similar shameful treatment, but chides Peter for not realizing that what looks like shame in human opinion does not at all reflect God's outlook.

Responsorial Psalm 116:1-2, 3-4, 5-6, 8-9

This late post-exilic psalm of thanksgiving makes a very fitting bridge between the first reading and the gospel in verse 6:

"The LORD keeps the little ones; / I was brought low, and he saved me." The psalmist was sick (close to death), maybe even in chains awaiting execution, but God rescued him. He was in sorrow, but now feels great joy. He experienced great insecurity, but now feels quite secure (feet won't stumble). For all of this he praises the Lord.

Twenty-Fifth Sunday in Ordinary Time
Wisdom 2:12, 17-20

In this section of Wisdom, the sacred author borrows images from Isaiah 52–66, specifically the fourth Servant Song (Isa 52:13–53:12), to illustrate how the Just One will be tested. The test, of course, is to see if the Servant will remain faithful, and whether God will indeed rescue him. Written about 50 B.C.E., this last book of the Christian Old Testament and today's verses in particular reflect the historical context quite well. Today's verses report the kinds of taunts apostate Israelites (those who abandoned the tradition) hurled at faithful Israelites who still awaited rescue from God, perhaps in the person of a Messiah. The verses are apparently intended to be associated with the first part of today's gospel in which Jesus reports his destiny for the second of three times in Mark's gospel (9:30-37).

Responsorial Psalm 54:3-4, 5, 6-8

The psalmist's very life is at stake, but he trusts in God who sustains life. The situation is urgent. Haughty and ruthless men seek his life, but the Lord sustains life. Grammatically, the Hebrew phrase describing God as one who sustains life indicates that that feature pertains to God's very essence: God is savior, rescuer, one who cares about and protects basic human existence. This sentiment characterizes the Old Testament reading and today's gospel.

Twenty-Sixth Sunday in Ordinary Time
Numbers 11:25-29

These verses describe the prophetic ecstatic trance that results from receiving the spirit, but they also report a concern about institutional control of prophecy. Yet since these people are not prophets in the strict sense but simply community leaders, it is clear that this is a once-for-all experience. The seventy received a share of Moses' spirit, hence these leaders were in a sense subordinate to Moses. The two men outside the camp received the spirit independently of Moses. They represent nonprofessional or "unofficial" prophecy. Joshua reflects those who would subject ecstatic trance to institutional control. He urged Moses to stop those two. Moses' reply is ambiguous. The Hebrew word can be translated jealous (Num 5:14, 30) or zealous (Num 25:11). The jealousy would pertain to the two "independent" prophets, zeal would of course pertain to safeguarding Moses' authority. Yet the further comment by Moses indicates that he would not at all want to restrict or control the power of God's energizing spirit. The congregation will benefit no matter who receives the spirit. It ought not be restricted to an elite group or a privileged few. As gift of God, the spirit should encounter no boundaries, limitations, or obstacles. Community leadership which does not heed prophetic insight can very likely lose its way and become misguided. The point of association between this reading and the gospel (Mark 9:38-43, 45, 47-48) is obvious.

Responsorial Psalm 19:8, 10, 12-13, 14

The Law in these verses represents all of Israel's directives and traditions as YHWH's chosen people. It is perfect, refreshes the soul, is trustworthy, bestows wisdom, is pure, endures forever, is true and just. Standing in the brilliant light of the Law, it becomes easier to notice one's shortcomings, unknown faults. Worse yet would be presumptuous (wanton) sins. The psalmist begs for protection against such.

Twenty-Seventh Sunday in Ordinary Time
Genesis 2:18-24

This familiar reading from the Yahwist reports God creating a fitting partner for the first human creature, the man. True to form, the Yahwist puts a pun in the man's mouth when he says "this one shall be called *'ishshah'* [woman], / for out of 'her *ish'* [man] this one has been taken." The next verse, Genesis 2:24, requires some cultural background for proper understanding. For millennia in the Middle East, the ideal marriage partner has been one's father's brother's daughter. See the stories of the Patriarchs, e.g., the story of how and from where Isaac's wife was selected in Genesis 24. In general, the men never leave the patriarchal household; they will always live with their father. Women, in contrast, must always move into their husband's household, which will be with his father. In a superficial reading Genesis 2:24 seems to contradict this practice: the man leaves father and mother and clings to his wife.

One needs to understand how families lived and continue to live in traditional settings in the Middle East. The extended family still remains the focal institution. Often it comprises part of a village or even an entire village. Male members dominate such family settings. The family may occupy a cluster of dwellings all under the leadership of the patriarch. One's father's brother will be living within this cluster of dwellings, hence so too will the ideal marriage partner be living there. In this context, an unmarried male can indeed leave the actual home of his father in which he has been living and move into his own dwelling with his father's brother's daughter living in the same complex. Here in this house he will cling to his wife and become one flesh without really leaving the wider family community (village?) over which the patriarch rules. The wife, too, enters the groom's father's domain without actually living under the same roof with her father-in-law. In today's gospel (Mark 10:2-16), Mark's Jesus cites Genesis 2:24 and reflects upon it (see John J. Pilch, *The Cultural World of Jesus Sunday by Sunday, Cycle B* [Collegeville: The Liturgical Press, 1996] 145–7).

Responsorial Psalm 128:1-2, 3, 4-5, 6

This personalized psalm begins with a macarism, often called a beatitude. Macarisms report approved cultural values along with the rewards for upholding the value. Since the core cultural value in the ancient Middle East is honor, the opening verse could be translated: "Truly honorable are you who fear the Lord." The psalm acclaims the joy such an honorable person will experience in labor, in the family setting, and indeed in all of Israel. It is a pilgrimage psalm sung for those departing Jerusalem, hence it functions as a blessing to accompany pilgrims on their journey home.

Twenty-Eighth Sunday in Ordinary Time
Wisdom 7:7-11

The Old Testament reading and the gospel have in common the notion of deeming wealth as nothing in comparison with more precious things such as Wisdom or discipleship and treasure in heaven. In our verses, the word "riches" signals an inclusion (vv. 8, 11), hence a unity for this text-segment intended by the author. Parallelism between "prudence" and "the spirit of wisdom" in verse 7 suggests that prudence be understood as "understanding." Solomon prayed for wisdom (1 Kgs 3:6-9) and preferred it to power, riches, health, comeliness, and light, yet these were given to him by God also. The man in today's gospel (Mark 10:17-20) obviously made a different choice.

Responsorial Psalm 90:12-13, 14-15, 16-17

Verse 12 is a prayer asking God to teach how to use time wisely in order to make the best use of a fleeting life. Verses 13-17 are a penitential prayer that God should extend steadfast loving-kindness to the psalmist so that God's deeds and honor (glory) might be witnessed by all. The psalm connects the Old Testament and gospel readings well with its petition for divine assistance in making wise choices.

Twenty-Ninth Sunday in Ordinary Time
Isaiah 53:10-11

Selected from the Fourth Servant Song (Isa 52:13–53:12), these verses proclaim eventual victory for the Servant which he never enjoyed in his lifetime. Recall that the Servant is Israel but dressed in the best values of Israel's heroes (Moses, Joshua, Samuel, Jeremiah). Yʜwʜ crushed Israel through the exile to Babylon. As a result, Israel lamented its sins and, because of this, will see light in fullness of days. Switching back from speaking about the community to speaking about Second Isaiah, Yʜwʜ notes that the innocent Servant will indeed justify the rest of Israel through his suffering. These Songs, like so many passages in the Bible, are rooted in the notion of collectivistic personality which characterizes 80 percent of the world's cultures, including that of the ancient Middle East. In such a perception, the individual has value and importance chiefly as a member of the collectivity, in this case, the people, Israel. The reading can be associated with the gospel (Mark 10:35-45) with the ideas that the Servant's suffering will justify many, as the Son of Man came to give his life as a ransom for many.

Responsorial Psalm 33:4-5, 18-19, 20, 22

The psalmist sees God's justice and right reflected in all of creation. More than that, the Lord looks from above with keen interest, steadfast loving-kindness, and mighty protection for those who show respectful fear. Those who place their trust in God will not be disappointed.

Thirtieth Sunday
in Ordinary Time
Jeremiah 31:7-9

Originally, this was an oracle about the restoration of the northern tribes. These verses describe a new Exodus. The very small "remnant" which escaped the Assyrian devastation of 721 B.C.E. now returns from exile, purified, to constitute a new Israel which will be faithful to God. This caravan includes people with no power (blind—the plausible link to today's gospel [Mark 10:46-52]—lame, mothers and pregnant women), thus indicating that only God could have liberated them. As in the original Exodus, Israel had water from a rock (Exod 17:1-7; Num 20:1-13); now God leads them along level roads to bubbling brooks.

Yet the language of these verses reflects Second Isaiah (blind, lame, mothers: Isa 35:5-6; God guides them: Isa 40:11; God gathers exiles: Isa 41:9; God leads this new exodus along a smooth and level road: Isa 40:3-5). Thus after the fall of Jerusalem in 587 B.C.E., Jeremiah probably reshaped an earlier oracle about the northern tribes and used the language of Temple liturgy to lift the spirits of the Exiles after the Temple had been destroyed. The final verse sounds a covenant theme. YHWH as father to Israel characterizes a covenant relationship. Actually it is a renewal of YHWH's love for Israel.

Responsorial Psalm 126:1-2, 2-3, 4-5, 6

The opening verses (1-3) reminisce about the return from Babylonian exile. Even Babylon now conquered by Persia was forced to acknowledge the power and graciousness of Israel's God. In this national lament, as in all laments, once Israel voices its grief, the priest responds with a word of hope: those that sow in tears shall reap rejoicing. And since this psalm was typically sung at the New Year, the beginning of the rainy season, the hope of rain which brings fertility to the fields is like a sign from God who will restore and enrich life for a repentant Israel.

Thirty-First Sunday in Ordinary Time
Deuteronomy 6:2-6

In the name of God, Moses presents a Law for life in the land. Deuteronomy repeatedly describes the land as "flowing with milk and honey" (see Deut 11:9; 26:9, 15; 27:3; 31:20), an image perhaps borrowed from Canaanite poetry, e.g., ANET 140: "The wadies fat with honey . . . flow with honey, etc."). The call to hear is also repeated often (Deut 5:1; 9:1; 20:3; 27:9), but on this occasion Israel is to hear the command to love YHWH alone. The cultural understanding of love is unflagging loyalty toward someone. In this case, love is rooted in covenant fidelity, basically a political idea. The client is expected to be devoted and loyal exclusively to the sovereign who selected and agreed to favor the client. Thus, "The LORD is our God, the LORD alone" is not so much (if at all) a profession of monotheism but rather an expression of exclusive loyalty and attachment to YHWH alone and to no others gods. The link between this reading and the gospel (Mark 12:28b-34) is obvious.

Responsorial Psalm 18:2-3, 3-4, 47, 51

Scholars believe that this song of thanksgiving may well be an authentic composition of King David himself. The opening phrase, "I love you," is actually spoken by God to Israel. The Hebrew word (*raḥam*, womb) never has God as its object in the Hebrew Bible, but that sentiment is frequently expressed by God toward the people. Then follow a string of titles applied to God: strength, rock, fortress, deliverer, shield, horn of salvation, stronghold. Many of these could be suggested to the author by the geography of the place where David's sanctuary and later Solomon's temple stood. The remaining verses are a personal statement of praise and thanks from the King to God for victory in battle.

Thirty-Second Sunday
in Ordinary Time
1 Kings 17:10-16

This is but one in a series of forty-five prediction-fulfillment stories spread through the course of 1–2 Kings which emphatically emphasize God's faithfulness in keeping promises. If God is so faithful in such small things, surely God will remain faithful to the great promise that David's dynasty will have no end. In Mediterranean cultural context, the story plays out in this fashion. It is a period of great drought predicted by Elijah who is obviously a man on intimate terms with God. The ever scarce food supply is even more scarce now. People live and survive in this culture by reciprocity chiefly between kin, which means mainly in the village. Villages tended to be one large, extended family. Hospitality to an outsider would be extended chiefly by a village leader. This is critical in the Middle East, a matter of life and death, because outside one's own village, one is considered a threat and could be killed were it not for the hospitality which grants safe passage. In this story, the widow has very scarce goods. In fact, the drought is so bad she fully expects to die along with her child very shortly; still the obligation of extending hospitality to the stranger is strong, even in the direst of circumstances. Elijah, the outsider, assures the widow that God will reward her kindness. From yet another cultural perspective, Elijah is truly an effective broker or intermediary with God, the widow's true and reliable patron.

No doubt, the "widow" links this reading with today's gospel (Mark 12:38-44). The widow with whom Elijah deals is hurt by the drought, but God comes to the rescue through the intervention of Elijah. The widow in the gospel is hurt by religious leaders who "devour the houses of widows," and Jesus, also an effective broker with God, publicly chastises the leaders and surely urges God to rescue that widow as well.

Responsorial Psalm 146:7, 8-9, 9-10

The psalmist sings praise to God who reliably provides for those whom society can not or will not help: the oppressed, the hungry, the captives, the blind, those bowed down, strangers, orphans, and widows. The wicked who are likely responsible for these disastrous experiences God will thwart. The congregation responds: Alleluia!

Thirty-Third Sunday in Ordinary Time
Daniel 12:1-3

These verses of Daniel conclude the revelation presented in chapters 10 and 11. Having traced Israel's sufferings and tribulations, Daniel notes that it is about to encounter the worst suffering of all times. Daniel is writing these chapters (10–12) around the years 167 to 164 B.C.E., reflecting the period of Antiochus Epiphanes' persecution. There is no indication how long this distress is going to last. The good news is, "your people shall escape," something which will occur with the death of Antiochus. "Your people" are very like the *hasidim*, the "pious ones" with whom Daniel identifies himself. It is very likely that Daniel is being very selective and referring only to the observant *hasidim*, those who shared his view of their contemporary experiences. (It is important not to confuse these *hasidim* with medieval and modern Jewish groups carrying the same name. The *hasidim* of Daniel's time opposed the Hellenization of Israelite thought and ways.)

Next we read the first and only unambiguous statement of belief in the resurrection of the dead in the entire Old Testament. Note that he says "many" and not "all." This probably reflects his conviction that it is only the observant members of his group, the *hasidim*, who will be so rewarded. These are the ones who suffered under Antiochus. Some shall live forever (or unto life everlasting, the first occurrence of this word in the Bible), but others to everlasting horror and disgrace.

Scholars are not in agreement on the interpretation of this phrase. If it is an antonym to everlasting life, what would "everlasting death" mean? And why should the dead be raised only to experience everlasting death? It does, however, fit the cultural pattern whereby people who feel that they are innocent but helpless are confident God will reward them. As for those who caused their problems, whom the innocent were unable to fend off while all were alive, well "you'll get yours, and God will give it to you!"

Finally, the wise (presumably Daniel and his fellow *hasidim*) will shine like the stars forever. The ancients believed that those who died took a place in the sky. Plato located them in the Milky Circle (= Way; *The Republic* 6.16, 29). Israelite tradition taught that the face of the elect would shine like the sun, and they would be like the light of the stars (4 Ezra 7:97). The mother of her martyred Maccabee sons is assured that her sons are already stars (4 Macc 17:4-5), having taken their place with the moon. As living beings, these celestial bodies (stars) continue to have impact upon human life. This is the reward for those who lead the many to justice.

Responsorial Psalm 16:5, 8, 9-10, 11

This lament is also a prayer of confidence by a Levite perhaps suffering from serious illness. The Levite expresses utmost confidence in God (his portion and his cup, cf. Jer 10:16; 51:19) who takes care of him. He keeps his attention focused completely on God. His heart (literally kidneys, the center of conscience and judgment), so long disquieted, will now rejoice. So too will his soul and entire body. As this psalm underwent development through frequent use in temple liturgies and by others, the sentiments also developed to reflect Israel's growing conviction that there would be some kind of survival after death in the eternal presence of God. Those are the sentiments of the final verse selected for today's response.

Thirty-Fourth Sunday
in Ordinary Time
(Christ the King)
Daniel 7:13-14

Daniel, like Ezekiel and John the Revealer, is an astral prophet in the Israelite tradition. This means that in ecstatic trance, an altered state of consciousness, these prophets analyze the constellations in the sky to discern God's will established there already at creation. The "one like a son of man" which Daniel sees is a constellation in human shape. The figure is not unlike the constellation that John the Revealer saw (Rev 1:13-16, quite likely Pleiades). Thus, a cosmic constellational son of man was quite familiar in the ancient Mediterranean world. Daniel then proceeds to interpret his vision.

Prior to this moment, he saw figures that resembled animals or beasts. Now he sees a human figure, a son of man. (It is not clear why the lectionary capitalizes "Son" in that phrase. The New American Bible translation does not capitalize that word.) Further, this human-like figure comes from God's realm, from the sky. Since the beasts represented pagan kingdoms, the human figure quite likely symbolizes a theocratic kingdom. To this figure, this kingdom, the Ancient of Days presents all the dominion previously possessed by the other kingdoms. Daniel, therefore, envisions the eventual appearance of a fifth monarchy. The son of man represents the saintly people of Israel.

Commentators correctly note that "kingdom" often seems to shift in Daniel into "king," which is what one would expect in a culture characterized by collectivistic personality and collectivist selves. In general, a collectivist self places group goals and concerns above individual goals and concerns. Collectivist self draws identity from and identifies with the group. (This is not the same as the "corporate personality" notion proposed by exegetes in the previous century. That notion was considered to be synonymous with "primitive mentality," something from which human beings would and should eventually evolve. Truth to tell, collectivistic personality characterizes 80 percent of the contemporary world population—including more than primitive peoples!) It was not difficult for later biblical tradition to shift the referent for the "son of man" from theocratic kingdom to an expected messianic king. It is at this point of our explanation that we can make an appropriate link to the gospel for today in which Jesus reflects upon kingdom and king (Mark 13:24-32).

Responsorial Psalm 93:1-2, 5

This is one of a series of psalms honoring YHWH as king and creator. The first two verses establish the cosmic setting; the "throne" of God is a constellation. Since God created all of this at the very beginning, it is obviously "from of old; / from everlasting." While this and other psalms were rooted in Canaanite mythology, Israel always "enculturated" what it borrowed. Verse 5 emphasizes obedience to God's covenant decrees. The result is that Israel will be holy because it complies with God's will. In this way, obedient and holy Israel will adorn the house of the Lord with holiness.

Recommended Readings

Old Testament

Craghan, John F. *Psalms for All Seasons*. Collegeville: The Liturgical Press, 1993.

Gottwald, Norman K. *The Hebrew Bible: A Socio-Literary Introduction*. Minneapolis: Fortress Press, 1985.

Holladay, William L. *Long Ago God Spoke: How Christians May Hear the Old Testament Today*. Minneapolis: Fortress Press, 1995.

Stuhlmueller, Carroll. *Psalms*. 2 vols. Old Testament Message. Wilmington, Del.: Michael Glazier, 1983.

_____. *The Spirituality of the Psalms*. Collegeville: The Liturgical Press, 2002.

Cultural World of the Bible

Pilch, John J. *The Cultural Dictionary of the Bible*. Collegeville: The Liturgical Press, 1999.

_____. *The Cultural World of Jesus Sunday by Sunday: Cycle B*. Collegeville: The Liturgical Press, 1996.

_____. *The Cultural World of the Apostles: The Second Reading, Sunday by Sunday, Year B*. Collegeville: The Liturgical Press, 2002.

_____. *The Triduum: Breaking Open the Scriptures.* Collegeville: The Liturgical Press, 2000.

Pilch, John J., and Bruce J. Malina, eds. *Handbook of Biblical Social Values.* Peabody, Mass.: Hendrickson Publishers, 1998.

Websites

Roman Catholic Lectionary for Mass:
http://clawww.lmu.edu/faculty/fjust/Lectionary.htm

Revised Common Lectionary:
http://divinity.library.vanderbilt.edu/lectionary